The French Revolution

Alan Forrest

BLACKWELL
Oxford UK & Cambridge USA

First published 1995
Reprinted 1996

Blackwell Publishers Ltd
108 Cowley Road
Oxford OX4 1JF
UK

Blackwell Publishers Inc.
238 Main Street,
Cambridge, Massachusetts 02142
USA

British Library Cataloguing in Publication Data
A CIP catalogue record for this book is available from the British Library.

Library of Congress Cataloging-in-Publication Data

Forrest, Alan I.
The French Revolution / Alan Forrest.
    p. cm. — (Historical Association studies)
Includes bibliographical references and index.
ISBN 0–631–18107–5. — ISBN 0–631–18351–5 (pbk.)
1. France — History — Revolution, 1789–1799.
        I. Title.   II. Series.
        DC148.F63 1995
        944.04 — dc20
                                                        94–9245
                                                        CIP

Typeset in 11 on 13 point Ehrhardt by Pure Tech Corporation, Pondicherry, India.
Printed in Great Britain by Hartnolls Ltd., Bodmin, Cornwall

This book is printed on acid-free paper

Historical Association Studies

The French Revolution

3

Historical Association Studies

General Editors: Muriel Chamberlain and H. T. Dickinson

China in the Twentieth Century
Paul Bailey

The Agricultural Revolution
John Beckett

Class, Party and the Political System
in Britain 1867–1914
John Belchem

Ireland 1828–1923: From Ascendancy
to Democracy
D. George Boyce

The Ancien Régime
Peter Campbell

Decolonization: The Fall of the
European Empires
M. E. Chamberlain

Gandhi
Anthony Copley

The Counter-Reformation
N. S. Davidson

British Radicalism and the French
Revolution
H. T. Dickinson

From Luddism to the First Reform
Bill: Reform in England 1810–1832
J. R. Dinwiddy

Radicalism in the English Revolution
1640–1660
F. D. Dow

British Politics Since 1945: The Rise
and Fall of Consensus
David Dutton

The Spanish Civil War
Sheelagh M. Ellwood

Revolution and Counter-Revolution in
France 1815–1852
William Fortescue

The New Monarchy: England
1471–1534
Anthony Goodman

The French Reformation
Mark Greengrass

Politics in the Reign of Charles II
K. H. D. Haley

Occupied France: Collaboration and
Resistance 1940–1944
H. R. Kedward

Women in an Industrializing Society:
England 1750–1880
Jane Rendall

Appeasement
Keith Robbins

Franklin D. Roosevelt
Michael Simpson

Britain's Decline: Problems and
Perspectives
Alan Sked

The Cold War 1945–1965
Joseph Smith

Britain in the 1930s
Andrew Thorpe

Bismarck
Bruce Waller

The Russian Revolution 1917–1921
Beryl Williams

The Making of Modern South Africa
Nigel Warden

Lloyd George
Chris Wrigley

The Historical Association, founded in 1906, brings together people who share an interest in, and love for, the past. It aims to further the study and teaching of history at all levels: teacher and student, amateur and professional. This is one of over 100 publications available at preferential rates to members. Membership also includes journals at generous discounts and gives access to courses, conferences, tours and regional and local activities. Full details are available from .The Secretary, The Historical Association, 59a Kennington Park Road, London SE11 4JH, telephone: 071–735 3901.

Contents

List of Figures

Select Chronology, 1787-1799

1787

22 February	Meeting of the Assembly of Notables
June–August	Refusal of Parlement of Paris to register royal reforms; exile of *parlementaires*

1788

8 May	Lamoignon's reforms to reduce power of *parlements*
7 June	'Journée des Tuiles' at Grenoble
8 August	Estates-General convened for 1 May 1789

1789

January	Disturbances caused by shortages of bread and firewood
March–April	Elections to the Estates-General
March–May	Popular revolts in Provence and Picardy
5 May	Opening of the Estates-General at Versailles
17 June	Third Estate declares itself to be the National Assembly
20 June	Tennis Court Oath
23 June	*Séance royale*: Louis orders the estates to meet separately

11 July	Dismissal of Necker
14 July	Taking of the Bastille
July–August	Peasant revolts and *Grande Peur* in many provinces
4 August	Abolition of privilege declared (though not yet enacted)
26 August	Declaration of the Rights of Man and the Citizen
6 October	March of the Parisian women on Versailles; royal family brought back to Paris
2 November	Clerical property placed at the disposal of the nation
14–22 December	Division of France into *départements* and *municipalités*
19 December	Creation of the first *assignats*

1790

January	*Jacqueries* in the Quercy and Perigord
13 February	Abolition of monastic vows
10 June	Request from Avignon for annexation into France
19 June	Abolition of nobility
12 July	Civil Constitution of the Clergy
14 July	Fête de la Fédération
16 August	Decree reorganizing the judiciary
18 August	First counter-revolutionary assembly at Jalès
31 August	Repression of army mutiny at Nancy
27 November	Decree enforcing clerical oath on public officials

1791

2 March	Suppression of the gilds
13 April	Papal bull condemning the Civil Constitution of the Clergy
14 June	Le Chapelier law banning workers' coalitions

20 June	Flight of the King to Varennes
17 July	Massacre on the Champ de Mars in Paris
4 August	First recruitment of battalions of volunteers
27 August	Declaration of Pillnitz
14 September	Louis XVI accepts the new constitution
14 September	Annexation of Avignon and the Comtat Venaissin
30 September	Dissolution of National Asembly
1 October	First meeting of Legislative Assembly
9 November	Decree against *émigrés* (vetoed by King 12 November)

1792

March	La Rouerie's conspiracy in Brittany
20 April	Declaration of war on Austria
27 May	Decree on deportation of non-juring priests (vetoed 19 June)
8 June	Decree establishing a camp of *fédérés* in Paris
12 June	Dismissal of Girondin ministers
20 June	First invasion of the Tuileries by the Paris crowd
11 July	Declaration of the 'patrie en danger'
25 July	Publication of the Brunswick Manifesto
10 August	Storming of the Tuileries and suspension of the King
19 August	Invasion of French territory by the Prussians
2–6 September	September Massacres in the prisons of Paris
20 September	Victory at Valmy
21 September	First session of the National Convention
9 October	Decree ordering death penalty for returned *émigrés*
6 November	Victory at Jemappes
11 December	First appearance of Louis XVI before the Convention

1793

16–18 January	Convention votes death of the King
21 January	Execution of Louis XVI
1 February	Declaration of war on Britain and Holland
24 February	New recruitment measures: the *levée des 300,000*
7 March	Declaration of war on Spain
9 March	Convention sends first deputies on mission to departments
10 March	Creation of special revolutionary tribunal
10–11 March	Massacres at Machecoul and start of Vendean insurrection
4 April	Defection of Dumouriez to the Austrians
6 April	Establishment of the first Committee of Public Safety
29 May	Insurrection against the Jacobin municipality in Lyon
31 May–2 June	Invasion of Convention by Paris sections; fall of Girondins
7 June	Federalist revolts in Bordeaux and the Calvados
18 June	Capture of Angers by the Vendeans
29 June	Defeat of the Vendean army outside Nantes
13 July	Assassination of Marat
17 July	Execution of Chalier in Lyon
27 July	Robespierre appointed to Committee of Public Safety
23 August	Decree on the *levée en masse*
27 August	Toulon handed over to the British navy
17 September	Law of Suspects passed
29 September	Introduction of the Maximum for grain and fodder
10 October	Revolutionary government decreed until return of peace
16 October	Execution of Marie-Antoinette
31 October	Execution of the Girondin leaders
24 November	Adoption of revolutionary calendar

4 December	Revolutionary government decreed: law of 14 *frimaire*
1794	
January	Repression in west; Turreau's *colonnes infernales*
February–March	Renewal of *chouannerie* in Brittany under Puisaye
26 February–3 March	Ventôse Decrees: sequestration of property of suspects and redistribution to the poor
4 March	Attempted insurrectio by Cordelier Club
13–24 March	Arrest and execution of Hébertistes
30 March–6 April	Arrest and execution of Dantonistes
8 June	Festival of Supreme Being in Paris
10 June	Law of 22 *prairial*: beginning of the Great Terror
26 June	Victory at Fleurus
23 July	Introduction of wage regulation in Paris
27 July	The ninth of thermidor: overthrow of Robespierre
28 July	Execution of Robespierre and Saint-Just
30–1 July	Reorganization of Committee of Public Safety
1 November	Hoche appointed commander of army in the west
12 November	Closure of Jacobin club
24 December	Abolition of General Maximum
1795	
1 April	Germinal: popular *journée* in Paris
5 April	Treaty of Basle with Prussia
April–May	Outbreaks of the White Terror in Lyon and the southeast
16 May	Peace signed with Holland
20 May	*Prairial*: invasion of Convention by Parisian crowd
24 May	Disarming of the Paris sections

21 July	Destruction of *émigré* army by Hoche at Quiberon
22 July	Peace signed with Spain
22 August	Convention adopts the constitution of the Year III
5 October	Vendémiaire: royalist rising in Paris
26 October	Dissolution of the Convention
3 November	Installation of the Directory

1796

19 February	Withdrawal of the *assignats*
2 March	Bonaparte appointed General-in-Chief of the Army of Italy
10 May	Conspiracy of the Equals; Babeuf arrested
December	Failure of Hoche's Irish expedition

1797

March–April	Royalist successes in legislative elections
27 May	Execution of Babeuf
4 September	*Fructidor*: coup d'état against the royalists in Paris
17 October	Peace of Campio-Formio between Bonaparte and Austria

1798

11 May	Removal from office of extreme royalist deputies
19 May	Bonaparte leaves on Egyptian Campaign
1 August	Nelson destroys French fleet at Aboukir Bay
5 September	Jourdan's law on military conscription

1799

March	War of the Second Coalition
April	Legislative elections favour neo-Jacobins
23 August	Bonaparte embarks for France

9–10 November	*Brumaire*: coup d'état brings Bonaparte to power
15 December	Proclamation of new constitution
25–7 December	Establishment of Council of State, Senate
28 December	Churches reopened for worship on Sundays

The Revolutionary Calendar

From about September 1793, as part of the process of dechristianization, the revolutionary authorities stopped using the Gregorian calendar and replaced it with their own system. This continued in use until well into the Empire. The year was divided into 12 months of 30 days apiece; and the months in turn were divided into 3 *décades*.

The following concordance gives the equivalent dates in the revolutionary and Gregorian systems for the Year II:

Month	Gregorian equivalent
Vendémiaire	*22 September–21 October 1793*
Brumaire	*22 October–20 November 1793*
Frimaire	*21 November–20 December 1793*
Nivôse	*21 December 1793–19 January 1794*
Pluviôse	*20 January–18 February 1794*
Ventôse	*19 February–20 March 1794*
Germinal	*21 March–19 April 1794*
Floréal	*20 April–19 May 1794*
Prairial	*20 May–18 June 1794*
Messidor	*19 June–18 July 1794*
Thermidor	*19 July–17 August 1794*
Fructidor	*18 August–16 September 1794*

As the year in the revolutionary system had only 360 days, the remaining 5 days were made up by the simple if rather clumsy expedient of using *jours complémentaires*. Thus, for instance:

20 July 1794 becomes 2 *thermidor* II
19 September 1794 becomes the *troisième jour complémentaire* of the Year II

1

Introduction

I should probably begin with a caveat. A short book of this kind
must necessarily restrict itself to a limited goal. In particular, it
would make no sense, in the small number of pages available,
to try to present yet another general history of the French
Revolution, especially since there are a number of excellent
general histories already available, in which the principal events
of the years from 1787 to 1799 are carefully dissected and in
which an overall interpretation of the Revolution is offered. My
aim here is a more modest one, that of analysing the nature of
the various changes which the Revolution wrought, social and
ideological changes as well as changes in political institutions.
The revolutionaries set out to destroy much of the infrastructure on which *ancien régime* France was built. But they were not
merely destructive, in spite of the overt vandalism of many
Jacobins. They also sought to create new institutions and new
social attitudes, to establish a new political and social order to
replace the old.

It is that process which is the principal subject of this book.
It concentrates on the Revolution itself, the ten years or so of
revolutionary administration which followed the calling of the
Estates-General and which were brought to a close by *Brumaire*
and the seizure of power by Bonaparte. It is not concerned with
the causes of revolution or with the collapse of Louis XVI's

1

government, nor yet with the conjunction of economic crisis and popular anger that marked the later 1780s. These issues are important in their own right, but they have been examined in great detail elsewhere, most especially during the last few years by William Doyle in his *Origins of the French Revolution* (Doyle, 1980). They are touched upon in Peter Campbell's essay in this series on *The ancien régime in France* (Campbell, 1988, pp. 71–82). And they have played a prominent part in the renewal of revolutionary studies, especially in this country and the United States, since the mid-1960s. But the question of causality is not the subject of this book, which will concentrate on the character of the revolutionary experience itself. How far did it overthrow the political order of the eighteenth century, as its leaders promised, and replace it with a truly revolutionary system of government? And to what degree did it succeed in carrying through the substantial social programme which it promised? Were the revolutionaries the victims of their own ideology and their own propaganda? Or should the whole episode be rated as a tragic failure, blown off course by religious intolerance, European war and insensitive centralism?

My aim, in short, is to suggest ways of viewing the revolutionary decade which may assist in an overall understanding of its achievements and ultimate failures. Those wanting a detailed general history of the period face an embarrassingly rich choice, representing very faithfully the historiographical battleground of the last fifty years. Georges Lefebvre and Albert Soboul presented, with differing degrees of directness and passion, the classic republican view which for most of the twentieth century monopolized opinion in France (Lefebvre, 1962–4; Soboul, 1974). Only relatively recently has that view been challenged in France, sometimes violently and often ideologically, by François Furet and others of his liberal and anti-Marxist persuasion (Furet, 1981, pp. 81–131). Yet, since Soboul's death in 1982, few can be found in France who will defend the republican orthodoxy or claim that 1789 was the great bourgeois revolution which ended the feudal order and paved the way for bourgeois power. His successor in the Chair

at the Sorbonne, Michel Vovelle, is an excellent social historian, by temperament close to the Annales school, and far more
attracted by the history of rural society, religious faith, and
social aspiration than by the transition from feudalism to
capitalism. In recent years he has become increasingly interested in the many representations and images of the French
Revolution, the theme he chose for the Bicentennial conference
in Paris (Vovelle, 1989, 1991, 1993). Even in eastern Europe
any consensus about the nature of the great French Revolution
is breaking down as ideological assumptions are swept aside. In
this country there never was a strong republican consensus of
the sort that existed, for quite understandable political reasons,
in France. Here the debate on the Revolution therefore took
very different forms. Lefebvre in particular commanded great
respect, but from the late 1950s the republican orthodoxy he
represented was being increasingly challenged. Historians such
as Norman Hampson shied away from any overall social
interpretation, stressing instead the intellectual foundations of
the revolutionary regime. For Richard Cobb, too, anything as
mechanistic as a dialectical approach was deeply antipathetic.
And Alfred Cobban's masterly exercise in academic scepticism,
The social interpretation of the French Revolution, was a significant nail in the Marxist coffin (Cobban, 1964, pp. 162–73). In
England the dominant historiographical current during those
years was a liberal one, which tended to concentrate its energy
on disproving the Marxist contentions about the French *ancien
régime* and the Revolution's place in world historical develop-
ment. Hence the strong emphasis on causation and the concentration not on the Revolution itself but on what went before.

The Bicentenary in 1989 has added mightily to the embar-
rassment of riches already at the student's disposal. In English
it produced two major general histories, those of William Doyle
and Simon Schama (Doyle, 1988; Schama, 1989). In France it
spawned a number of valuable publishing enterprises, including
a range of historical dictionaries of the revolutionary period and
an excellent atlas, the various volumes of which are still
appearing. It created a new general interest in the Revolution,

at least temporarily, through intense media coverage: François Furet in particular became something of a cult figure in France, and the school of intellectual historians which he leads gained considerable acclaim well beyond the narrow circle of revolutionary specialists. The preparation of the Bicentenary also created during the last years of the 1980s a huge amount of more specialized publication, much of it on the cultural history of the period, and brought scholars together to participate in a rich panoply of conferences and colloquia, both in France and across the world. Much of the cost was funded by a French government anxious to identify with the cause of the Rights of Man and a President, François Mitterrand, who made the celebration of 1789 into something of a personal crusade. The Bicentenary was at once a scholarly enterprise and a political statement, a slightly uneasy mixture of analysis and celebration. Both aspects reached their zenith on Bastille Day, 14 July. The Congrès Mondial brought scholars from all over the world to a week-long conference at the Sorbonne, while popular enthusiasm was harnessed by the daring tableaux of the sumptuous Bastille Day procession along the length of the Champs-Elysées.

France could not afford to ignore the Bicentenary, even if, in 1989, some of the associations of the Great Revolution – the Jacobin dictatorship, the Terror, state centralism, religious intolerance – were no longer as acceptable to republican opinion as they had been a hundred years earlier. The Revolution was a part of the country's political heritage, an event which not only contributed to France's international reputation but which helped provide the republican tradition with a degree of legitimacy at home. French people can still identify with their Revolution to a degree that is impossible for foreigners, though François Furet is right to suggest that the degree of that identification has significantly weakened since the early 1970s. A socialist government steeped in the radical traditions of the nineteenth century saw it as its mission to reawaken a fading public awareness and as its political interest to identify with the best aspects of what the Revolution stood for. But whereas in

1889, at the time of the centenary, republicans insisted that the whole Revolution was above criticism, François Mitterrand and his advisers were more circumspect. Egalitarianism did not always create positive associations, and too great an insistence upon legislative centralism could have seemed sadly at odds with the Europe of the late 1980s. After all, 1989 was not only the year of the Bicentenary. It was also the year when the centralist regimes of eastern Europe were being systematically challenged and their assumptions rejected by a large segment of their populations, the year which would see the final demolition of the Berlin Wall. All of this might suggest that the legacy of the French Revolution has not escaped unscathed, and that its libertarian message has survived the passage of two centuries rather better than its egalitarian one.

In both the analysis of historians and the public discourse of politicians it was clear how much had changed since 1889, between the Third Republic and the Fifth. In 1889 the deputy for the Aube, Jean Casimir-Périer, could proclaim unambiguously that the ideas of the revolutionaries had lost none of their force. 'The new nation will listen because it is convinced', he told a great banquet at Vizille, 'forgive because it is strong, wait because it is young.' And, he went on, 'the future belongs to the sort of society which the Revolution has moulded: the future belongs to the Republic which, in the political order, is the final consecration of the work which our forebears achieved' (Nieto, 1988, p. 177). The principles of the Revolution, he declared unambiguously to an ecstatic audience of believers, remain our principles today. Those scholars, such as Aulard and Mathiez, who were appointed to the newly founded Chair in the history of the French Revolution at the Sorbonne, would find little in that statement with which to disagree. They remained profoundly loyal to a radical or socialist vision of France. Aulard, it is true, tended to identify his vision of the Revolution most closely with Danton, Mathiez with Robespierre. But the differences in their outlook were far less significant than the similarities. They both saw the Revolution as the genesis of the secular, anti-clerical republicanism in which they devoutly believed. Their admiration for the Revolution and their belief in the Republic were as one.

In 1989, in contrast, neither politicians nor historians were prepared to make such an unqualified statement of faith. In the run-up to the Bicentenary some historians expressed open hostility to the Revolution and to what they saw as the lasting damage which it had done to French society. On the right, for example, historians like Pierre Chaunu and Reynald Secher were bitter in their condemnation of the revolutionaries, denouncing their inherent brutality and identifying the First Republic not with generous ideals but with the 'genocide' of the civil war in the Vendée (Secher, 1986, introduction by Chaunu, p. 24). Among politicians, too, many had little interest in celebrating the achievement of the Revolution, while those, like Mitterrand, whose loyalty was to the revolutionaries, were at pains to make clear just how far that loyalty stretched. The President's public utterances spoke of a revolution that had been carefully sanitized: there were no references to the power of the state, to centralization, to the tiresome conflicts between Church and state which had so delighted the radicals of a hundred years before. There were very few acknowledgments of the ideal of equality. Instead François Mitterrand's revolution concentrated prudently on those things which divided French people least – the individualism of 1789, the civil rights guaranteed for the citizenry, the freedom of worship for Protestants and Jews, the Declaration of the Rights of Man and the Citizen. Therein, seen through the highly selective lens of the Bicentenary, lay the very essence of the French Revolution.

It would be difficult to claim that the Bicentenary has created any new interpretation or established any new orthodoxy. Public celebrations of its kind seldom do. But the work of historians during the 1980s, much of it published in and around the period of the Bicentenary, has moved on from some of the old debates and obsessions of the previous generation. If the Marxist paradigm of a revolution moving France from feudalism to capitalism is for all purposes dead, so interest in the classic 'revisionist' arguments about the causes of 1789 has also fallen away. In a sense that is because there was no longer a debate to pursue, so completely has the historiographical landscape shifted. But in another sense the very concept of 'revisionism' had always been flawed, a label which neither the Marxists nor their opponents much liked and which has now outlived all semblance of usefulness. The academic treatment of the Revolution is much healthier in the 1990s for being more open, arguably more confused, certainly less entrenched in rival encampments.

Since the early 1980s much of the most vigorous historical scholarship has been in the area of political history, where Furet, Keith Baker and others have insisted on the primacy of political motivation within the French Revolution. But their definition of what constitutes political history is not the same as that of historians even ten or twenty years before. Political forms and processes received new investigation, with a surge of interest in clubs, popular societies, newspapers, pamphlets, elections and political symbolism. Since the language of revolution was political, greater attention has been given to that language, to the discourse of revolutionary politics, in an attempt to elucidate its meaning for contemporaries. In the process the attention of scholars has tended to shift from those periods of the Revolution when free expression was stifled – in particular, from the Year II and the Jacobin republic – to those when discussion was relatively free, when the nature of the revolution was still being determined by rival groups of conservatives and constitutionalists, radicals and patriots. And since the majority of those who took a leading part in constitution making and major policy decisions during the period of the National and Constituent Assemblies were themselves members of the enlightened elite of the last years of the *ancien régime*, the Enlightenment and the process of politics during the late eighteenth century have themselves achieved a new vogue. Historians such as Keith Baker and Lynn Hunt in the United States are less interested in the day-to-day events of revolutionary politics than in something much wider which they term political culture. Hunt has no doubt of its central importance to contemporaries. 'The chief accomplishment of the French Revolution', she argues, 'was the institution of a dramatically new political culture' (Hunt, 1984, p. 15). I leave it to Baker himself to explain this concept, which plays a major part in much modern political writing on 1789. 'If politics, broadly construed, is the activity through which individuals and groups in any society articulate, negotiate, implement and enforce the competing claims they make upon one another, then political culture may be understood as the set of discourses and practices characterizing that activity in any given community' (Baker, 1987, p. xii). It was one of the principal tasks of the revolutionaries, discarding as they did many of the accepted norms of political conduct during the ancien régime, to create for themselves a new revolutionary order, a new and distinctive political culture.

The emphasis on culture has largely squeezed out the concern for class, since political culture can be presented as part of a wider process, that of creating what Mona Ozouf has termed '*l'homme nouveau*', a new, regenerated, revolutionary human being, purged of the egoisms and cultural attitudes of the *ancien régime* (Lucas, 1988, p. 213). New cultural assumptions had to be transmitted, new values inculcated if the Revolution were to succeed, and the multiple processes which this implied have been scrutinized not just by historians, but by anthropologists, linguisticians, art historians and others. Artists – not just the greatest of them, Jacques-Louis David, but the thousand or so artists who practised their craft in the midst of the Revolution and who came to terms with the new rhetoric of the period – are given a new importance. For art, like language, can tell us a great deal about the underlying social and ideological assumptions of the age. So can the music of the period, much exploited in the symbolic festivals of the revolutionary years; here there is a considerable change from the liturgical works of 1789 and 1790 to the deeply committed operas of André Chénier. The festival itself became an art form, that of the Supreme Being one of David's greatest revolutionary inventions, and the Jacobins were well aware of the power of images like the altar of the fatherland, the tree of liberty, or the *bonnet rouge* of the *sans-culottes*. Lynn Hunt has examined the symbolism of patriotic images, the competing representations of radicalism in the gendered symbolism of Hercules and Marianne (Hunt, 1984, pp. 87–119). James Leith has shown the importance of religiosity in French revolutionary culture, whether in the fervour of patriotic ceremonial – often an overt imitation of Church practice – or in the luminosity of its iconography (Leith, 1989, pp. 171–85). And for many revolutionaries, attracted by the power of words, language itself became a cultural tool, the repeated use of iconographic expression a form of persuasion and a catalyst to conformity. Rhetoric had its own symbolism; and words could lead to actions. As early as 1789 Sieyès talked of the radical novelty of the Revolution's political language; by 1793, notes Jacques Guilhaumou, that language had become the *langue du peuple*, placing 'political language at the heart of Revolutionary knowledge and of Jacobin political knowledge in particular' (Guilhaumou, 1989, p. 118). Revolutionary culture depended intimately on such representation: the book, the pamphlet, the press, all became parts of a powerful cultural crusade to reform mentalities and chase out the last vestiges of the *ancien régime*.

If the political history of the period has been so dominant, what of social history? Because the old social history was so closely entwined with the feudalism-to-capitalism orthodoxy, there was always a danger that the attack on the Marxist-republican model would bring with it a rejection of any social view of the French Revolution. In France, as Steven Kaplan reminds us, François Furet has gradually widened his offensive against Marxism to include any form of social interpretation of 1789 (Kaplan, 1993, p. 734). He is not alone in this. In the Anglo-Saxon world, too, some historians seek to deny that the Revolution had any true social dimension. Simon Schama, for instance, argues in *Citizens* that 'the drastic social changes imputed to the Revolution seem less clear-cut or actually not apparent at all', adding for good measure that the bourgeoisie, once portrayed as the motor force of revolution, 'have become social zombies, the product of historiographical obsessions rather than historical realities' (Schama, 1989, p. xiv). Even if he is right – and many will dismiss his words as crudely polemical – does it mean that all the social policy making of the revolutionary years was little more than empty posturing? Social historians may not have proposed any new post-Marxist synthesis to explain the Revolution, but that does not mean that the social and economic history of the period is condemned to irrelevance. Even in time of revolution politics is not everything, and too single-minded a concentration of political discourse is itself a form of reductionism. It is true, of course, that the Marxist school of historians overplayed the social impact of the Revolution in their quest for a satisfyingly universal formula. But that does not mean that it had none. If the language of the Revolution was unfailingly political, much of the action of the revolutionary assemblies was aimed at ending social wrongs – inheritance laws, legal privilege, land tenures, corporate structures. These were not chance gestures, tangential to the sense of the Revolution as a whole; rather they must be seen as central to the purpose of a movement that had ambitions to promote social as well as political change.

Much new work continues to be produced on the social fabric of France during the Revolution, bringing fresh approaches to bear on the subject. Historians of the Revolution are more concerned with the history of *mentalités*, of collective attitudes and popular culture. There have been studies of the peasant revolution, of agriculture, forests and commons, of village politics and local identity. The nature of religious belief has been re-examined as has the character of village politics. The popular movement has been analysed in terms that artisans and journeymen might have understood, in terms of neighbourhood bonds and the language and culture of the workplace. The place of women and the family has been given a new prominence. The history of the Revolution in provincial France has been largely rewritten. In the process social groups and social identities have been redefined, the nature of loyalties re-examined. Historians have looked at the effects of war and militarization, at revolutionary expansionism beyond France and the changes which that wrought upon the Revolution itself. And they have examined the various forms of opposition to Paris which marked the 1790s, some ideological, the majority cultural in inspiration. Nor, with so much interest in history from below, have elites been forgotten. There is a notable project currently under way in Paris to analyse the lot of the middle classes during the Revolution, the commercial and professional groups who had often shown such dissatisfaction with the structures of the *ancien régime*. And the concept of a revolutionary bourgeoisie, though more broadly defined than in the past, has not been wholly eclipsed. In 1990, indeed, Jean-Pierre Hirsch made a timely plea for the bourgeois to be rehabilitated. They played, he believes, an important role throughout the Revolution, which found them 'more attentive, better educated, better equipped than the others to face up to the unexpected'. Within a few months of the calling of the Estates-General 'they were everywhere: at Versailles and in Paris, but also in the new municipalities and militias, members of corresponding societies, editors of newspapers, men responsible for provisioning. . . . The Revolution was bourgeois inasmuch as the bourgeois gained the greatest advantages from it (increasing particularly, through the purchase of national lands, its share of the principal resource, the land).' It was also bourgeois, believes Hirsch, in that the bourgeois could and did help define the new political order and assumed an essential role in the political direction of the country (Hirsch, 1990, p. 237). Their importance should not be overlooked.

From this new research no single model or paradigm has emerged to replace the one which has been swept aside. This may be no bad thing. The French Revolution was not, after all, a single, tidy entity, coherent in its objectives from 1789 through to Brumaire. No one in the France of 1788 or 1789 planned the Revolution that was about to break out around them, and many of the initiatives of the revolutionary years were little more than expedients devised to deal with short-term crises such as food shortages or the flight of the King.

Besides, the meaning of the Revolution was very different for peasants and businessmen, soldiers and artisans; and it meant different things depending on whether one lived in Paris or Perpignan, Lyon or the Vendée. It is only right that the history of the period should reflect something of that diversity, of the desperation and, on occasion, anarchy which characterized it. So recent historiography is not, in my view, any poorer for being more diffuse, even if it does not lend itself easily to synthesis. Indeed, as Colin Lucas has remarked, 'when one thinks back to the premisses that held sway thirty years before, one can only conclude that French Revolution studies have become immensely richer and more exciting' (Lucas, 1991, p. vii). If this book communicates to its readers even a small fraction of that excitement, it will have succeeded in its central purpose.

2

1789

The background to the Revolution

During the last years of the *ancien régime* there was widespread dissatisfaction, at many different levels of society, with the manner in which France was being governed. But that dissatisfaction did not of itself cause the overthrow of absolute monarchy. Rather it was the severity of the financial crisis of the 1780s, triggered by France's costly participation in the American War of Independence, which made the continuance of the status quo an unattainable aim. By the later 1780s even many of the privileged members of society were prepared to concede that they must sacrifice some of their privileges if the monarchy and the social system were to survive. It is true that the various reform programmes proposed by the King's ministers were in turn rejected, leaving the monarchy without a clear economic policy and threatening to plunge the country into bankruptcy. But this cannot be blamed solely on the intransigence of the privileged orders of society. The debates of the last years of the *ancien régime* were not only about money. They were about the rights of property, about privilege, about the definition of liberty. What was at issue was less the necessity of reform than the price that should be exacted for such reform: if the nobility were not wholly opposed to increasing their

13

contribution to the costs of running the state, if they were prepared to make a contribution to salvaging an increasingly desperate financial deficit, they were also intent on having a greater say in how the money should be spent, and determined to curtail the absolutist ambitions of the monarch. In the Parlement of Paris and the twelve provincial *parlements* the privileged orders maintained their pressure on the King. Any financial concessions that they might make would have a considerable political price. For that reason the economic crisis of the 1780s was soon turned into a political crisis, a crisis about power, representation and royal authority.

This same perception was displayed in many of the *cahiers de doléances* that were drawn up throughout France, by privileged and unprivileged alike, in the months before the Estates-General met. Not all the *cahiers* were revolutionary in their content. Nearly all declared themselves in favour of the King and of the maintenance of the monarchy. Some, indeed, saw the greatest need as that of re-stating old constitutional rights which had been eroded during the years of royal absolutism, the liberties of cities and provinces, the freedoms granted by provincial constitutions. Bayonne, for instance, demanded that the free-port status it had gained by royal charter must be protected; and the nobles of Aix-en-Provence cited the virtues of what they termed their Provençal constitution. But, as François-Xavier Emmanuelli has shown, there was no such constitution; the document to which they referred was little more than a collection of texts built up since the Middle Ages establishing a certain number of privileges and forming the basis for regional power. Like many provincial nobles, theirs was a deeply conservative plea (Emmanuelli, 1977, p. 129). Among the Third Estate, however, demands were often mre radical. Their confidence in the monarchy might remain intact, but they expected the King to prevent the abuses of ministers, of intendants, of tax collectors. And many went further, asking for representation and demanding the abolition of hated taxes and feudal dues on which the political and social system was founded. What is more, the very process of drawing up a *cahier*, of being asked to express grievances, of learning that the document was to be passed on to a more central authority so that the King and the Estates-General could take note of the people's views, aroused expectations which would not subsequently fade away. To that degree, at least, Tocqueville was right to view the *cahiers* as presenting a fundamental challenge to the legitimacy of the old order.

The demand for reform

If there was widespread demand for reform in 1789, there was little to suggest violent revolution. Louis himself might be unpopular, not least in Paris, criticized for his indecisiveness and scorned for his sexual impotence; and the widespread hatred of Marie-Antoinette did little for his personal standing. But the institution of monarchy was seldom questioned. Few in 1789 spoke the language of equality or of democracy, and those who did, like Sieyès and Mirabeau, were treated with suspicion. Political expectation was more modest. When the Estates-General met on 5 May it was, of course, accepted that they would address political as well as financial issues. If the King wanted financial concessions, this was the moment when the *parlements*, the estates, the people could hope to demand something in return which might guarantee them a permanent place in the councils of the realm. The estates, and especially the Third Estate, were eager to extract concessions, to control what they saw as the abuses of absolute monarchy, but their ambitions stopped there. The dominant figures of the Third Estate during the summer months of 1789 were almost all committed monarchists, men like Mounier, Lally-Tollendal, Bergasse and Clermont-Tonnerre, who wished to prevent any overt attack on the executive power of the King. They were the men who were in charge of the drive for constitutional reform, and they would dominate the constitutional committee established by the National Assembly. The cause of reform, it seemed, was safe in their hands, the perils of revolution safely averted.

But what reform? The expressions of consensus and the euphoric welcome reserved for the Rights of Man during the heady summer of 1789 often obscure the fact that there was no easy reform package that could resolve the structural problems of the French monarchy. The experience of the previous decade made that very clear. Neither the false optimism of Jacques Necker in 1781 nor the abortive reform programmes presented by Calonne and Brienne in the years that followed had provided an answer to the financial weakness of the Crown; the national debt was too great, and the cost of servicing that debt too punishing, for limited reforms to have any chance of success. And if the apparent opulence of court life provided radical pamphleteers with an easy target, the real problem lay far deeper, in the whole construct of privilege and the fiscal base of the state. Eighteenth-century French society, like its government, was predicated upon a corporate structure; people were not individuals but representatives of various interests and legal estates. Hence there was little room for tinkering, little place for moderation, unless that moderation could reform the whole corporate basis of *ancien régime* society. In this sense Calonne's proposals of August 1786 could be regarded as highly revolutionary; they sought not only to overhaul the tax system but also to reform the *pays d'élections* and remodel the administrative machinery of the state. In particular, they advocated a system of provincial assemblies which would draw no distinction between the three estates, or between privileged and non-privileged – a system which was intended to reduce the influence of the lay and clerical nobility in local affairs and which betrayed a disregard for privilege that ran counter to the social norms of the *ancien régime* (Goodwin, 1953, p. 29). The notion that the monarchy could adapt to the new economic circumstances without leaving a trail of pain and destruction was both dangerous and illusory.

In the event, of course, the optimism of men like Malouet and Mounier proved terribly misplaced. They failed to take account of the new mood in Paris and leading provincial cities, a mood which had been moulded by the very public debates of 1787 and 1788 on the nature of the polity and which the summoning of the Estates-General itself helped to implant. Nor did they take account of the acrimony of the struggle between monarchy and nobility which had dominated French politics during these years. Faced with the need to gain approval for his reform plans, the King had tried to bypass the *parlements* by calling an Assembly of Notables to meet at Versailles in February 1787. But this proved to be a serious miscalculation, just as his Chancellor, Miromesnil, had warned, for the Assembly did not give Louis the pliant support he was seeking. Indeed, not only did the Notables try to impose greater controls on state finances; they also stressed the need for constitutional proprieties, insisting that any fiscal reforms must be approved by either the Parlement or by an Estates-General. In its turn, the Paris Parlement refused to register the decree, demanding that an Estates-General be summoned for the first time since 1614 to deal with the crisis. The King in anger responded by exiling the *parlementaires* to Troyes on 15 August, and a campaign of heightened bitterness followed, with Louis vacillating unconvincingly between rigidity and compromise. Even once he had granted their principal demand, the calling of the Estates-General, mutual suspicion persisted, and 1788 was marked by bitter battles between King and Parlement over the registration of edicts, the use of *lettres de cachet*, and the legality of *lits de justice*. By the time the Estates-General met, both sides had unleashed a powerful war of propaganda, and if there was agreement on the double representation of the Third, there was little agreement on anything else. The Estates-General assembled in an atmosphere of expectation and high tension.

That expectation was not confined to Paris. The demand for reform, as had been proved in the Dauphiné in 1788, was a heady cocktail, one which affected the ordinary people of Grenoble as much as the assembly of the three orders of Dauphiné which met on 21 July at Vizille. The violence of the

Journée des Tuiles provided a timely reminder that ideas of representation and anti-seigneurialism could not easily be contained (Chomel, 1988, pp. 63–94). Elsewhere, regional loyalties often focused on the *parlement*, especially where – as in Paris, Pau and Bordeaux – it had been in conflict with royal authority. Enthusiastic crowds filled the streets when the *parlementaires* returned triumphantly from exile. Indeed, throughout much of the country the political temperature rose dramatically. The *cahiers* played a notable part in this process, giving men at every level of society the chance to vent their anger and express their grievances. It mattered little that these grievances often went only to the local *bailliage*; people convinced themselves that they would be acted upon, that they would be read by the King. And, as Tocqueville commented, what they demanded amounted to little less than the overthrow of the existing order. The elections through which the deputies were chosen also helped to crystallize opinion and to raise expectation. In Paris and in many provincial centres a new political class was in the process of being born. In this process the printing press and the increased levels of literacy in the population at large played a substantial part. For these crucial months were marked by a flurry of pamphleteering and the launch of a cascade of newspapers, many of them lasting only a few weeks but helping to create a new culture, at least in the cities, which was receptive to the discourse of politics. The scribblers of Robert Darnton's Grub Street suddenly found fame and appreciation, as their captions and caricatures were reproduced on wall bills and their more inflammatory outbursts read to groups of artisans in bars and wine shops (Darnton, 1982, pp. 1–40). This sudden explosion of political tracts was symptomatic of a new consciousness among the urban population. It helped create a mood of excitement, particularly in Paris, which would be difficult for the authorities to control and which made it most unlikely that the work of reform could be contained within the Estates (Gough, 1988, pp. 15–36).

When the deputies met, it was soon clear that no amount of royal pressure would restrict them to budgetary issues. Discussion turned quickly to matters of procedure. In particular, there was the vexed issue of how the different estates should meet and vote, an issue which had not been crisply resolved when the Estates-General were called. The Third, in recognition of the size of their constituency, had been given twice the representation of the other two orders. But they had not been granted what was widely seen as the more crucial concession, the right to vote by head and not by order so that every vote would not be reduced to a meaningless contest over the retention or abolition of privilege. In contrast to the situation in 1614, when the Estates-General had last met, the Third Estate of 1789 had acquired a robust sense of its own importance. 'What is the Third Estate?', the *abbé* Sieyès had asked rhetorically in what was probably the most influential pamphlet among the two and a half thousand published before 1789. It was, he argued, 'everything', represented in all the key areas of French business and professional activity. Yet its political influence in the past had been minimal, a situation which, Sieyès claimed, it was the duty of the Third's deputation to reverse. The King, by ordering them to meet in the time-honoured manner, compelled the deputies to make their first vital choice. They could either obey their monarch and admit that their numbers and economic strength gave them no real voice in politics. Or they could throw down a challenge to royal authority, a challenge which, by its very nature, would transform the nature of political discourse and launch France on the path to revolution. It was an issue on which one side or the other had to give way, and had to be seen to give way. There was no room for compromise.

The issue was a crucial one, and not merely because of the King's opposition. For this was not an empty question of procedure. Opinion among the deputies of the First and Second Estates was more fluid than might have been expected; both the clergy and the nobility contained within their ranks some notable disciples of change. Hence if they met as a single body, voting without distinction of orders, the Third could hope to win over converts and advance the cause of reform.

The liberal thinking of the Enlightenment, the debates in provincial academies and masonic lodges, the acrimonious relations between King and Parlement during the previous twenty or thirty years, and the extraordinarily democratic electoral procedures which Louis had authorized for the choice of deputies all helped to create a body that was open to reform. The deputies who assembled at Versailles were not all obsessed with the interests and status of their order; what united and divided them was often ideology, the way in which they regarded institutions and social structures. The model of America was there before them – Lafayette himself was already a popular hero in Paris – as a society which had successfully created liberal political institutions, while many of the men of 1789 regarded Britain with a degree of envy, as a country which had favoured individualism and which had, as a result, flourished both politically and economically. In all there were 1,201 deputies, of whom 610 represented the Third Estate; and the other two orders each contained a quota of liberals on whose support the Third came increasingly to depend. Among them were some fifty liberal nobles, some of whom would go on to make their mark upon revolutionary politics. And many of those representing the First Estate were country *curés*, whose grievances were often directed at the bishops and abbots within their own order. If the Third Estate won and a single assembly was formed, those committed to reform could hope to command a working majority. Radicals and conservatives alike were aware that this was the crucial issue and that it had to be resolved one way or the other.

The manner of its resolution gave a considerable fillip to the cause of the radicals, men like Sieyès and Mirabeau and the future mayor of Paris, Bailly. The Third took refuge in what seemed to be a procedural gambit, refusing to verify its elections until the other two orders joined it in a common assembly. This was, as Peter Campbell points out, a clever tactic, since it placed the initiative with the privileged orders and, at one remove, with the King (Campbell, 1988, pp. 80–1). After weeks of uncertainty the existing structure began to crumble. On 10 June the Third invited the privileged members to join them, adding – the idea was that of Sieyès – that those not present when a roll-call was taken of all 1,201 deputies would be regarded as being in default. Between the 12th and the 14th that roll-call was indeed taken, showing that only a handful of parish priests had responded to the invitation. But the Third did not allow themselves to be deterred. On 17 June they declared themselves to be the National Assembly, with the proclaimed aim of providing France with a constitution; and they at once took the step of confirming existing taxes, at least provisionally. All deputies were urged to join them, to fuse the three orders into one single body. On 19 June there was a significant breakthrough when the majority of the clergy declared themselves in favour of meeting as one assembly, a move which drove the bishops to appeal to the King. On the following day the political temperature was raised yet again, when the Third found themselves locked out of their chamber; it was widely believed that the King intended to dismiss the Estates-General, if necessary by force. The deputies retired to an adjoining tennis court to decide on their next move. They could have backed down, fearful of royal anger and the threat of a *lit de justice*. Instead they chose to defy the King, reasserting their right to form a national assembly without distinction of order and binding themselves to their decision by the Tennis Court Oath. It was a gesture of defiance that united all factions within the Third Estate; one solitary deputy declined. The oath was proposed by Mounier and drafted by three other leading lawyers, Target, Barnave and Le Chapelier; Bailly was the first to swear (Goodwin, 1953, p. 58). And it placed the initiative squarely with the King. In the eyes of many historians it was a vital moment, one that transformed the political character of 1789 and pushed France towards open revolution.

The deputies took considerable personal risks in defying the King's authority, and they were well aware of these risks. Each and every one of them was called upon to take the oath personally, placing his own individual safety in jeopardy and sheltering uncertainly behind the strength which numbers could convey. 'We swear', they each intoned, 'not to separate, and to reassemble wherever circumstances require, until the constitution of the kingdom is established and consolidated upon firm foundations; and that, the said oath taken, all members and each one of them individually shall ratify this steadfast resolution by signature' (Stewart, 1951, p. 88). They did so fully aware that their defiance could be destroyed by a single act of royal authority. But how would Louis respond? He came under competing pressures from his closest advisers, Necker urging that he make real concessions to mollify the Third Estate, while Barentin pressed for incisive action to break their rebellion. When the court returned to Versailles on 21 June the King's brothers, Provence and Artois, made clear their opposition to reform, and Necker's cause was lost. At the *séance royale* on the 23rd Louis gave his reply. He made few real concessions of moment. His tone, it is true, was conciliatory as he promised the deputies some limited reforms: personal liberty, freedom of the press, and the power to consent to taxes. But his statement was received in almost total silence, for he made no concessions on the vexed matter of the moment, insisting that the orders continue to meet separately in three chambers. And he made it clear that he intended the social fabric of the *ancien régime* to be upheld. The entire session, says Goodwin, 'bore the character partly of a *lit de justice* and partly of a military *coup de force*' (Goodwin, 1953, p. 59). It is difficult to disagree, or to see the *séance royale* as other than a precious opportunity recklessly thrown away.

When the King left the hall, the deputies of the Third refused to follow, Bailly articulating the defiance of them all when he claimed that 'the assembled nation cannot receive orders' (Lefebvre, 1962, p. 114). On this as on other occasions Louis had offered too little to appease his opponents and appeared grudging at a time when only generosity could have harnessed public sympathy. But neither did Louis have the strength of his convictions. In the days that followed the privileged orders accepted the King's ruling and met in their separate chambers, the clergy finally constituting themselves on

o fear. But it would be misleading to stop there
e that popular insurrections were devoid of all
vation. In Paris the people would soon produce
ders with their distinctive political programmes;
l bills and posters, were harangued by journalists
from the Palais Royal, and mingled political
h their cries for adequate bread supplies and
ces. A new role was being carved out for the press
nd campaigning journalists used newspapers to
 own political causes. Radicals stirred popular
nore stylish and polemical forms of journalism:
'89 Parisians could choose between Brissot and
larat and Desmoulins. In the countryside, too,
t anger led to violent confrontation, there was
note of anti-seigneurialism as well as a demand for
a and country alike, the heightened expectations
ne calling of the Estates-General raised political
 and encouraged people to believe that something
e to assuage long-standing grievances.

round to the popular revolution was economic
ng the reign of Louis XVI almost every area of
uction had suffered grievously during what Ernest
ntified as a series of cyclical depressions. Wine-
heir prices fall by as much as 50 per cent in the
d when prices recovered it was only because of
nallholders and sharecroppers were the principal
 being reduced to beggary and near-starvation. In
in prices fell sharply, before a series of poor
87, 1788 and 1789 cut supply and pushed prices
h many consumers could not afford to pay. And
80s drought and cattle disease brought disaster to
mal husbandry. Peasant culture is dependent on
lity, prices and yields which may be modest but
 fluctuate too far, weather conditions that follow
 the agricultural year. The sheer unpredictability
before 1789 was what drove many peasants to
d ate up both their reserves and the seedcorn for

the 25th. But there was little sense of security, and both
ministers and deputies were increasingly alarmed by the threat
of disorder. There was talk of a mob of thirty thousand
Parisians invading the palace and trying to impose a national
assembly by force. Fearful of popular mobilization a small
number of deputies from the First and Second Estates broke
ranks and joined the Third. And Louis had no stomach for civil
war. On 27 June he reversed his decision of the 23rd, ordering
the remaining members of the privileged orders to meet in a
single chamber. The National Assembly was granted the recognition it sought; the Third had achieved a major political
revolution, thanks in large measure to the indecision and
vacillation of the Court throughout the weeks of the Estates-
General's existence.

What gave the National Assembly its sense of purpose during
the days that followed was neither class interest nor political
sectarianism. Rather it was a desire to protect individual rights
against repression, a desire which pitted the new political class
against the corporatist principles on which eighteenth-century
France was constructed. Gilds, associations and privileges –
even those accorded by the state – were perceived as the enemy
of an individualism which, as Patrice Higonnet has argued,
became the pivotal force in both social and political life
(Higonnet, 1981, pp. 1–6). Freedoms of movement and trade,
expression and conscience were to be paramount, and the
deputies believed that clear constitutional guarantees were
needed if these were not to be lost. By 7 July they had
appointed a constitutional committee; on the 9th Mounier
delivered its first report and the Assembly had added 'constituent' to its title. But the path was not yet clear for a liberal
victory. The court had hesitated, but the royalist factions had
not given up hope of reversing the drive towards constitutionalism. On the 11th, the day on which Lafayette submitted his
draft for a declaration of human rights, Louis responded with
a measure which seemed to many liberals to threaten all that
had been achieved. He dismissed his principal minister,
Necker, who enjoyed a wide measure of popular trust,

banishing him from the kingdom and replacing him by the reactionary baron de Breteuil. With a ministry of men he could trust, arch-conservatives and supporters of absolutist ideas, many feared that it was but a short step to military intervention and the dispersal of the Assembly by force.

The popular revolution

This fear helped to mobilize the Paris crowd and to inspire what Georges Lefebvre termed the 'popular revolution'. Most historians now regard Lefebvre's rather mechanistic division of the different forces which contributed to the 1789 revolution as terribly simplistic: in *The coming of the French Revolution*, published just before the Second World War, he argued that there were four separate movements which contributed to the overthrow of the *ancien régime*, respectively an aristocratic, bourgeois, peasant and popular revolution, with each playing its own distinctive role (Lefebvre, 1939). Few would accept that interpretation today, with its implication that each group acted out of discrete class interests rather than from any sense of political commitment. Liberal nobles and commoners shared many of the same political and ideological outlooks, to the extent that they can be seen as a common interest group even in an age of privilege. The nobility, as Guy Chaussinand-Nogaret reminds us, was a dynamic group, many of them attracted to investment in new capitalistic enterprises as well as in mining and banking ventures and in the modernization of their estates. 'Contrary to a widespread opinion nobles were not forbidden to engage in trade, and the Crown, above all from the time of Colbert who complained of not being able to find investors for his overseas trading companies, had issued and reissued edicts designed to encourage nobles to turn to commercial activities' (Chaussinand-Nogaret, 1985, p. 92). Equally, in the pursuit of offices and honours, there was little to distinguish nobles from the upper echelons of trade and the law. Rich merchants aped the aristocracy, living nobly on their

country estates and seekin
eenth-century respectability
professional elites impervic
gilds and corporations were
nomic well-being and of the
Bossenga has phrased it ir
Lille, they were at once a
advancement, and quasi-au
from their statutes and reg
their own realm the gildsr
maintenance of privilege j
Versailles. Both groups prov
frightened of any assault i
also produced men deepl
Enlightenment, prepared to
mitted to ideas of natural

Any view of 1789 which
and fast social lines is ther
divisions counted for at lea
where people thought of th
class terms. This is not, o
tion in its entirety: in t
periods, economic grieva
easily acquire political im
still has some validity for
complex and rapidly chan
the idea that there was ir
brought together constit
Norman peasants and Pa
swept aside. For if liberal
elite, those educated grou
the new ideas of the ag
shaped by the literature
Rousseau, by Turgot and
explain the violence of the
countryside the people w
shortages, while their pr

rumour a
or to ass
political r
their own
they read
and agita
demands
affordable
as engage
advance t
opinion by
already in
Loustallot
where pea
often a cle
food. In to
aroused by
consciousn
could be d
The bac
misery. Di
primary pr
Labrousse
growers sa
late 1770s,
low yields.
victims, ma
the 1780s
harvests in
to levels w
in the mid-
regions of a
a certain sta
which do n
the seasons
of the year
destitution a

future years. In many regions of France the economic future seemed desperate. Yet the peasants had been asked their views in the *cahiers*; they had often informed the King of their plight. And in the elections for the Estates-General they had received promises of a less unjust and better regulated world. In the summer of 1789, at exactly the time when the Estates-General met in Paris, granaries were empty and prices were rising rapidly. For the poorer peasants, like the urban workers consumers rather than sellers of grain, the summer months brought only hunger and misery until the new harvest could be brought in. Economic hardship served to kindle their resentment and turn many of them to acts of violence and destruction.

Peasant resentment was not wholly economic, though economic anger helped fuel other discontents. In many parts of France there were long-standing social tensions between privileged and unprivileged, between those rich enough to store grain and exploit the market and those whose poverty meant that they were permanently at its mercy. These tensions were increasing during the eighteenth century, when rising population and increased pressure on land further depressed the condition of many poorer peasants. The growth of commerical towns brought in its wake a socially aggressive merchant class who were eager to buy land in the surrounding countryside, further squeezing the amount of land available for local people. Viticultural regions like Aquitaine saw extensive replanting in vines: with every year that passed more cornfields were ripped out and more peasant proprietors dispossessed as land was given over to the high-quality *grands crus* which made the Bordelais famous throughout northern Europe. And as Robert Forster has shown, the move to a more efficient, more capitalistic approach to land management was not confined to rich *roturiers* or to the *anoblis*. The old nobility in areas like the Toulousain were just as attracted by new management ideas, just as prepared to override traditional peasant practices (Forster, 1960). Their capitalist approach, their desire to ensure a return on their investment, contrasted with traditional peasant concerns for stability and inheritance. Such innovation, whether by noble estate owners or by merchant *arrivistes*, was seen by many local people as an unwelcome intrusion into the culture of their rural world.

If peasants faced a challenge from the new culture of investment and profitability, they also faced increased demands from more traditional sources. Levels of royal taxation were perceived as being unbearably heavy, and in many parts of the kingdom this was probably true, though regional studies point to the huge discrepancies between local practice rather than to any clear overall trend. What can probably be said is that the poorer peasantry, those without a surplus to sell, were very badly affected by increases in indirect taxation, and that the gross inequalities between province and province, even between village and village, caused anger and outrage. And, as Peter Jones has stressed, the widespread feeling that tax levels were rising focused discontent on tax exemptions, and hence on the whole question of seigneurialism (Jones, 1988, p. 42). Feudal dues, too, were a common source of anger amongst the peasantry, who could not see why they were expected to make money payments and perform labour services when they were getting little that was tangible in return. They were not social revolutionaries: as the *cahiers* make plain, few would have challenged the notion of privilege, which remained an essential part of their world picture. But they were increasingly resentful of payments which brought no benefit either to themselves or to their communities – tithes to a Church which spent them on court fopperies when the parish church was in disrepair and the local hospital derelict, feudal exactions which helped sustain the conspicuous consumption of the idle rich. In years of poor returns the cumulative weight of these dues became crippling, especially where payments had to be made in kind rather than in cash. Besides, for many peasants the sums demanded were increasing in real terms during the last years of the *ancien régime*. The extent of this so-called 'feudal reaction' has sometimes been exaggerated, but for those most directly affected it was a source of burning resentment, as nobles attempted to maintain their lifestyle by increasing levels of payment and the 25th. But there was little sense of security, and both ministers and deputies were increasingly alarmed by the threat of disorder. There was talk of a mob of thirty thousand Parisians invading the palace and trying to impose a national assembly by force. Fearful of popular mobilization a small number of deputies from the First and Second Estates broke ranks and joined the Third. And Louis had no stomach for civil war. On 27 June he reversed his decision of the 23rd, ordering the remaining members of the privileged orders to meet in a single chamber. The National Assembly was granted the recognition it sought; the Third had achieved a major political revolution, thanks in large measure to the indecision and vacillation of the Court throughout the weeks of the Estates-General's existence.

What gave the National Assembly its sense of purpose during the days that followed was neither class interest nor political sectarianism. Rather it was a desire to protect individual rights against repression, a desire which pitted the new political class against the corporatist principles on which eighteenth-century France was constructed. Gilds, associations and privileges – even those accorded by the state – were perceived as the enemy of an individualism which, as Patrice Higonnet has argued, became the pivotal force in both social and political life (Higonnet, 1981, pp. 1–6). Freedoms of movement and trade, expression and conscience were to be paramount, and the deputies believed that clear constitutional guarantees were needed if these were not to be lost. By 7 July they had appointed a constitutional committee; on the 9th Mounier delivered its first report and the Assembly had added 'constituent' to its title. But the path was not yet clear for a liberal victory. The court had hesitated, but the royalist factions had not given up hope of reversing the drive towards constitutionalism. On the 11th, the day on which Lafayette submitted his draft for a declaration of human rights, Louis responded with a measure which seemed to many liberals to threaten all that had been achieved. He dismissed his principal minister, Necker, who enjoyed a wide measure of popular trust, banishing him from the kingdom and replacing him by the reactionary baron de Breteuil. With a ministry of men he could trust, arch-conservatives and supporters of absolutist ideas, many feared that it was but a short step to military intervention and the dispersal of the Assembly by force.

The popular revolution

This fear helped to mobilize the Paris crowd and to inspire what Georges Lefebvre termed the 'popular revolution'. Most historians now regard Lefebvre's rather mechanistic division of the different forces which contributed to the 1789 revolution as terribly simplistic: in *The coming of the French Revolution*, published just before the Second World War, he argued that there were four separate movements which contributed to the overthrow of the *ancien régime*, respectively an aristocratic, bourgeois, peasant and popular revolution, with each playing its own distinctive role (Lefebvre, 1939). Few would accept that interpretation today, with its implication that each group acted out of discrete class interests rather than from any sense of political commitment. Liberal nobles and commoners shared many of the same political and ideological outlooks, to the extent that they can be seen as a common interest group even in an age of privilege. The nobility, as Guy Chaussinand-Nogaret reminds us, was a dynamic group, many of them attracted to investment in new capitalistic enterprises as well as in mining and banking ventures and in the modernization of their estates. 'Contrary to a widespread opinion nobles were not forbidden to engage in trade, and the Crown, above all from the time of Colbert who complained of not being able to find investors for his overseas trading companies, had issued and reissued edicts designed to encourage nobles to turn to commercial activities' (Chaussinand-Nogaret, 1985, p. 92). Equally, in the pursuit of offices and honours, there was little to distinguish nobles from the upper echelons of trade and the law. Rich merchants aped the aristocracy, living nobly on their

country estates and seeking that ultimate accolade of eighteenth-century respectability, ennoblement. Nor were France's
professional elites impervious to notions of privilege. Their
gilds and corporations were the defenders both of their economic well-being and of their status in the community. As Gail
Bossenga has phrased it in the context of pre-revolutionary
Lille, they were at once a source of 'social rank, professional
advancement, and quasi-autonomous political authority derived
from their statutes and regulations' (Bossenga, 1991, p. 6). In
their own realm the gildsmen of Lille had an interest in the
maintenance of privilege just as entrenched as the nobles at
Versailles. Both groups provided their share of arch-conservatives,
frightened of any assault upon their power. But both groups
also produced men deeply committed to the ideals of the
Enlightenment, prepared to fight against fiscal privileges, committed to ideas of natural rights.

Any view of 1789 which sees political conflict following hard
and fast social lines is therefore likely to be flawed. Intellectual
divisions counted for at least as much as social ones in a society
where people thought of themselves in corporate rather than in
class terms. This is not, of course, to discount social explanation in its entirety: in the eighteenth century, as in other
periods, economic grievances were deeply rooted and could
easily acquire political importance. Lefebvre's vision of 1789
still has some validity for historians trying to make sense of a
complex and rapidly changing political landscape. In particular,
the idea that there was in 1789 a conjunction of forces which
brought together constitutional lawyers and liberal nobles,
Norman peasants and Parisian woodworkers, cannot be easily
swept aside. For if liberalism could unite large sections of the
elite, those educated groups who had been exposed to some of
the new ideas of the age and whose views had come to be
shaped by the literature of the day, by Montesquieu and
Rousseau, by Turgot and the Physiocrats, it can do little to
explain the violence of the popular revolution. In Paris as in the
countryside the people were partly driven by hunger and food
shortages, while their propensity to violence owed much to

rumour and to fear. But it would be misleading to stop there or to assume that popular insurrections were devoid of all political motivation. In Paris the people would soon produce their own leaders with their distinctive political programmes; they read wall bills and posters, were harangued by journalists and agitators from the Palais Royal, and mingled political demands with their cries for adequate bread supplies and affordable prices. A new role was being carved out for the press as engaged and campaigning journalists used newspapers to advance their own political causes. Radicals stirred popular opinion by more stylish and polemical forms of journalism: already in 1789 Parisians could choose between Brissot and Loustallot, Marat and Desmoulins. In the countryside, too, where peasant anger led to violent confrontation, there was often a clear note of anti-seigneurialism as well as a demand for food. In town and country alike, the heightened expectations aroused by the calling of the Estates-General raised political consciousness and encouraged people to believe that something could be done to assuage long-standing grievances.

The background to the popular revolution was economic misery. During the reign of Louis XVI almost every area of primary production had suffered grievously during what Ernest Labrousse identified as a series of cyclical depressions. Wine-growers saw their prices fall by as much as 50 per cent in the late 1770s, and when prices recovered it was only because of low yields. Smallholders and sharecroppers were the principal victims, many being reduced to beggary and near-starvation. In the 1780s grain prices fell sharply, before a series of poor harvests in 1787, 1788 and 1789 cut supply and pushed prices to levels which many consumers could not afford to pay. And in the mid-1780s drought and cattle disease brought disaster to regions of animal husbandry. Peasant culture is dependent on a certain stability, prices and yields which may be modest but which do not fluctuate too far, weather conditions that follow the seasons of the agricultural year. The sheer unpredictability of the years before 1789 was what drove many peasants to destitution and ate up both their reserves and the seedcorn for future years. In many regions of France the economic future seemed desperate. Yet the peasants had been asked their views in the *cahiers*; they had often informed the King of their plight. And in the elections for the Estates-General they had received promises of a less unjust and better regulated world. In the summer of 1789, at exactly the time when the Estates-General met in Paris, granaries were empty and prices were rising rapidly. For the poorer peasants, like the urban workers consumers rather than sellers of grain, the summer months brought only hunger and misery until the new harvest could be brought in. Economic hardship served to kindle their resentment and turn many of them to acts of violence and destruction.

Peasant resentment was not wholly economic, though economic anger helped fuel other discontents. In many parts of France there were long-standing social tensions between privileged and unprivileged, between those rich enough to store grain and exploit the market and those whose poverty meant that they were permanently at its mercy. These tensions were increasing during the eighteenth century, when rising population and increased pressure on land further depressed the condition of many poorer peasants. The growth of commerical towns brought in its wake a socially aggressive merchant class who were eager to buy land in the surrounding countryside, further squeezing the amount of land available for local people. Viticultural regions like Aquitaine saw extensive replanting in vines: with every year that passed more cornfields were ripped out and more peasant proprietors dispossessed as land was given over to the high-quality *grands crus* which made the Bordelais famous throughout northern Europe. And as Robert Forster has shown, the move to a more efficient, more capitalistic approach to land management was not confined to rich *roturiers* or to the *anoblis*. The old nobility in areas like the Toulousain were just as attracted by new management ideas, just as prepared to override traditional peasant practices (Forster, 1960). Their capitalist approach, their desire to ensure a return on their investment, contrasted with traditional peasant concerns for stability and inheritance. Such innovation, whether by noble estate owners or by merchant *arrivistes*, was seen by many local people as an unwelcome intrusion into the culture of their rural world.

If peasants faced a challenge from the new culture of investment and profitability, they also faced increased demands from more traditional sources. Levels of royal taxation were perceived as being unbearably heavy, and in many parts of the kingdom this was probably true, though regional studies point to the huge discrepancies between local practice rather than to any clear overall trend. What can probably be said is that the poorer peasantry, those without a surplus to sell, were very badly affected by increases in indirect taxation, and that the gross inequalities between province and province, even between village and village, caused anger and outrage. And, as Peter Jones has stressed, the widespread feeling that tax levels were rising focused discontent on tax exemptions, and hence on the whole question of seigneurialism (Jones, 1988, p. 42). Feudal dues, too, were a common source of anger amongst the peasantry, who could not see why they were expected to make money payments and perform labour services when they were getting little that was tangible in return. They were not social revolutionaries: as the *cahiers* make plain, few would have challenged the notion of privilege, which remained an essential part of their world picture. But they were increasingly resentful of payments which brought no benefit either to themselves or to their communities – tithes to a Church which spent them on court fopperies when the parish church was in disrepair and the local hospital derelict, feudal exactions which helped sustain the conspicuous consumption of the idle rich. In years of poor returns the cumulative weight of these dues became crippling, especially where payments had to be made in kind rather than in cash. Besides, for many peasants the sums demanded were increasing in real terms during the last years of the *ancien régime*. The extent of this so-called 'feudal reaction' has sometimes been exaggerated, but for those most directly affected it was a source of burning resentment, as nobles attempted to maintain their lifestyle by increasing levels of payment and

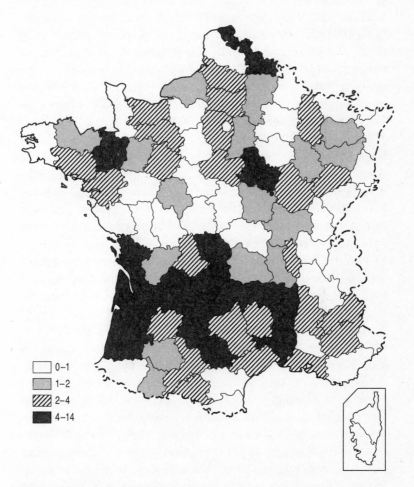

Figure 1 Intensity of anti-feudal troubles, by department
Source: Anatoli Ado; reproduced in M. Vovelle, *La Découverte de la politique* (Paris: La Découverte, 1993).

scouring their archives to resurrect forgotten obligations. The belief that nobles were exploiting their traditional prerogatives helps explain the violent anti-seigneurial feelings that characterized certain regions of France during 1789.

That violence was often propelled by panic. Panics were frequent occurrences in the French countryside, as rumours spread from hamlet to hamlet and the fear of hunger, repression or military reprisals engulfed whole regions of the country. Steven Kaplan has written eloquently about the prevalent belief in famine plots among the communities of the Paris Basin, where, as recently as 1775, serious rioting was sparked off by the belief that the people were being deliberately starved by their political oppressors (Kaplan, 1982, pp. 1–4). The Great Fear which affected large areas of France between December 1788 and March 1790 falls easily into the tradition of such famine plots, with the local aristocracy often cast in the role of the wicked oppressor, resisting the changes that were being discussed and legislated and trying to starve their peasants into a passive acceptance of their lot. As with most fears, it is difficult to offer any coherent or logical explanation of the course which it took. Most outbreaks of fear remained localized and resulted from reports of the alleged sightings of 'brigands', men of rough appearance, strangers to the locality, ruthless bands of desperate criminals who would put the countryside to the sword. That, at least, is how they were described by terrified villagers; but it would seem that it was the fact that they were strangers, men travelling far from home, *gens sans aveu* impoverished and in rags, desperate for sustenance, that attracted the notice of local people. Wild rumours spread rapidly, mobilizing the rural population against all outsiders and those who did not enjoy their trust. Whole communities armed themselves, often led, as in the Quercy and the Périgord, by rural artisans with the tacit support of the wealthier farming community (Boutier, 1979, pp. 769–70). The presence of Parisians, of soldiers, of people from another province who spoke with an unfamiliar accent, any disruption of customary norms could provoke panic in a highly volatile countryside. In

July 1789 fearful rumours spread through the Ile-de-France and the parishes of the neighbouring provinces. Villages, markets, isolated farmsteads were being threatened by 'brigands', market riots were taken as evidence of a famine plot, and local people rushed to take arms. As Georges Lefebvre has shown, the creation of a bourgeois militia in Paris in the summer of 1789 itself became the cause of fears elsewhere, as farming communities imagined themselves infested with the undesirables of the capital. The panic spread rapidly from town to town and into the smallest villages of the Ile-de-France. On 14 July it reached Sceaux, on the 16th Suresnes, on the 19th Gonesse and Santeny-en-Brie, on the 21st Chevilly and l'Hay, on the 22nd Marcoussis (Lefebvre, 1932, p. 150). The hinterland of Paris was soon scored with the fault lines of rumour, unease and panic.

Though there was nothing so coordinated as an insurrectionary movement in the French countryside, and though almost all parts of the country were at one time or another affected by incidents of collective violence, the Grande Peur was largely concentrated in some six or seven areas. These ranged from Hainault and Lower Normandy in the north, through Alsace, Franche-Comté and Dauphiné in the east, to Provence and Aquitaine in the south. Some experienced little more than spasmodic outbreaks of panic, often directed at beggars making their way to or from Paris; in other cases, and especially in the south west, the fear rapidly assumed an anti-seigneurial dimension. Nobles, it was believed, were organizing the brigand bands in order to demoralize the people and to deprive them of their hard-won political rights. In consequence, the rioting became more political in character, with the insurgents turning their anger on the *châteaux*, the granaries and the persons of the *seigneurs* themselves. Castles were stormed, seigneurial documents seized and burned, landlords and estate managers assaulted. In some parts of the country – most notably, perhaps, in the Agenais and the Périgord – the insurrections gave vent to long-standing social hatreds, justifying the claim of the Soviet historian Anatoli Ado that peasant violence in the summer of 1789 'placed the question of feudal dues at the very forefront of the social struggle in the country-side' (Ado, 1987, p. 132). This was violence on a scale that had not been witnessed in rural France for many years. It spread panic among the propertied classes and among their repre-sentatives on the Estates-General and the National Assembly. It drove some nobles to emigrate; others, more conciliatory to the wishes of the people, were convinced by the rumours of social anarchy which daily reached the capital that now was the time for compromise rather than confrontation. Rural violence was a vital element in explaining the willingness of the privi-leged orders to join with the Third. It helped seal the victory of the National Assembly. It also promoted the spirit of renunciation which broke out in that assembly during the night of 4 August, when many of the privileged orders, intoxicated by the mood of reconciliation and national unity, made impas-sioned speeches laying down their privileges and declaring their belief in the universal brotherhood of man.

If violence in the countryside helped to cement the victory of the Third Estate, so did violence in the streets of Paris. Here, too, food shortages helped focus discontent and catalyse unrest. Paris had, after all, a long tradition of bread riots, the most recent of them in 1775. Like the poorer peasants, the people of the capital were predominantly consumers for whom bread was the main staple, the yardstick by which they judged their well-being. Shortages brought with them high prices and empty shops, and the sight of the rich buying stocks of high-quality bread while their own families starved drove many shoppers to violence and revolt. Besides, urban consumers were much given to plot theories, to believing rumours that the nobility, the Court, and the greater grain merchants were in league to force up prices by holding back supplies. Merchants, millers and grain wholesalers were all suspect in periods of shortage. Hoarders and speculators were a traditional target of popular wrath, and crowds would attempt to impose a popular or just price for the goods, a price that fell ludicrously below what the market demanded. Stallholders regarded this practice – known as *taxation populaire* – as little different from theft, but for the people of the capital it had its own morality, even its own legitimacy, in times of deprivation. Unlike the politicians in the National Assembly, they had no reason to like the idea of a free market, the promise that prices would be fixed by the interplay of supply and demand. They increasingly repeated their demands for some form of price control, their demand that the government guarantee their right to eat. These demands reached a peak in the spring and early summer of 1789, when the price of bread had risen to a point where it was consuming as much as nine-tenths of a journeyman's wage (Soboul, 1974, pp. 136–7).

Bread is not, of course, the whole story. The people of Paris, like those of Lyon, Marseille and other large cities, cannot be categorized only as consumers, at the mercy of price movements and mobilized solely by hunger. They had their own culture, their daily routine of work and leisure, their characteristic dress, their tradition of heavy drinking. And that culture was, in its own distinctive way, imbued with values and with politics. Long traditions of corporate activity ensured that artisans and tradespeople of the capital understood the extent of their political muscle and were accustomed to fight for their rights, whether literally, in the *compagnonnages* – the confraternities to which young workers traditionally belonged – or more figuratively, through the gild structure and the courts. If they did not share any sense of class identity, in the sense in which the term would be understood in a later industrial age, they were united by their corporate identity, by the traditions of their trade and the fraternity of the workplace. In addition, as David Garrioch has shown for Paris, the popular classes were united by other structures which influenced their behaviour and informed their day-to-day existence, by family and friendship networks, by region of origin, by neighbourhood and a sense of local community (Garrioch, 1986, pp. 16–55). In provincial cities like Grenoble and Marseille the existence of such traditions would play an important part in the process of radicalization; in Grenoble, for instance, workmen and artisans had been prominent in the violence of the Journée des Tuiles in June 1788. But in Paris popular violence, and with it the culture of the streets and the workplace, would be on an altogether larger scale. The fact that Paris was the seat of government gave its population far greater opportunity than in any provincial centre to have a direct effect on political events, and Parisians were fully aware of the power which this conveyed. In 1789, when the Estates-General met, it is true that journalists and popular agitators fanned out from the Palais Royal into the popular areas of the city, stirring up hopes and focusing anger. But the people whom they harangued were already imbued with their own notions of equity and justice, their family values, their sense of popular morality.

From the spring of 1789 violence always threatened as bread prices soared inexorably. In April an outburst of popular anger and looting followed rumours of wage cuts, and one of the largest factories in the capital, Réveillon's wallpaper works, was attacked. By July, with bread at 14 sous per pound, tension had reached a new peak, and the dismissal of Necker, who retained a certain popularity among ordinary Parisians, unleashed a new wave of rioting. Rumours spread that the move heralded a new aristocratic conspiracy, and popular radicals used the opportunity to arm themselves and to mobilize the people. On 13 July barricades were thrown up in the streets. Gunsmiths' shops were looted and weapons seized. Tollgates were sacked. On the 14th the crowd attacked the Bastille, the hated royal prison and fortress which stood, threatening and lowering, between the Faubourg Saint-Antoine and the city. In the ensuing battle over one hundred men were killed by troops defending the fortress, and when the governor, de Launay, finally surrendered, the confused and impassioned crowd fell upon him, murdered him and paraded his head – along with that of the *prévôt des marchands*, Flesselles – through the city on a pike. For the people of the capital the fall of the Bastille was a moment of intense symbolism, when they had by their own efforts toppled a monument to royal authority. Those who had fought and died in the assault became overnight heroes of the crowd. But for the propertied classes, for repectable Paris and for the deputies, the symbolism was far more menacing. For them the attack on the Bastille was a symbol of anarchy and disorder which demonstrated the power of popular insurrection. It convinced many of the need to progress through constitutional reform. And it played a major part in deciding the waverers among the deputies to cross the floor and recognize the new National Assembly. Yet again the action of the people had cemented the achievement of the liberal revolution (Godechot, 1970, pp. 267–73).

This lesson was not lost upon the radical leaders in Paris. They saw that they, too, had a role to play, a view which was given still more weight in October when another crowd, composed mainly of the women of the Paris markets, marched to Versailles and brought the royal family back to the Tuileries. Once again the people had acted decisively, and by reducing the King's freedom of manoeuvre they had given new impetus to the Assembly and to the programme of reform. Their part in the unfolding drama of 1789 was a significant one, and one that had not been written in the original script. The intentions of the legislators had been to control the reform movement and to limit political participation to the propertied classes, yet already the more radical among them were looking to the streets and markets of the capital to give added strength to their cause. The lesson of these summer months was clear, that for many Frenchmen the unleashing of controls and the proclamation of new freedoms was only the beginning. Many began to take initiatives of their own, challenging the traditional local structures in the name of the Assembly and of revolutionary liberty. In various provincial cities that summer was marked by a so-called 'municipal revolution', often provoked, like the Parisian disturbances, by Necker's dismissal and a consequent feeling that the King had betrayed them. Without any legal authority other than the moral authority which the Revolution itself conferred, the old municipal bodies coopted local notables or handed over their powers to the electors. They looked to the Assembly for a lead, not to the King. They enjoyed far more autonomy from the centre and took pride in ordering municipal affairs. Often they took command of a bourgeois militia or national guard, defending their town against both the aristocracy and the peasantry of the surrounding countryside.

In the few months between the calling of the Estates-General and the October Days the political configuration of France had changed utterly. No longer could Louis XVI realistically believe that he was an absolute monarch, however poorly he understood some of the forces unleashed against him. He was still King, of course, but was he sovereign? The revolutionaries increasingly talked of sovereignty as residing not in the person of the monarch but in the collectivity of the French people, the nation. The Revolution that emerged during these months had its own ideology, its own liberal and individualistic ideals. In the economic sphere the ideas of the Physiocrats had already made sizeable inroads into mercantilist thinking during the 1770s and 1780s, but now economic individualism emerged as an essential aspect of the liberty of mankind. Restrictions, prerogatives, what the eighteenth century had described as liberties, these had little impact on revolutionary thinking. Nor could the privileged and corporate groups of the *ancien régime* assume that their traditional privileges would continue to be respected. Liberal values, as enshrined in the Declaration of the Rights of Man of 26 August, informed many of the government's actions, and individualism was regarded as a healthy antidote to government controls and constraints. Politically, too, the victory of the moderate constitutional monarchists seemed assured, and with the renaming of the assembly as the Constituent Assembly, its main purpose was to draw up a liberal constitution for France. The deputies, it seemed, had emerged from their first uncertain steps in June to establish an undoubted political primacy over the country. The nature of the new political order seemed to be in the process of being defined.

Yet already in 1789 there were threats to any supposed consensus. It assumed the cooperation of the King, and there were ominous signs that that could not be taken for granted.

Louis might not openly oppose the Revolution, but he was clearly disenchanted by many of the changes, while Marie-Antoinette's hostility was well known. Some at least of the aristocracy were already convinced that there was no place for them in the new order, a France where the public rhetoric was openly hostile to both the nobility and their traditional values. Large numbers were already looking beyond the frontiers of France, to emigration, and they included a high proportion of the country's army officers, a career that had been largely restricted to the nobility during the last years of the *ancien régime*. The response of the Church, too, was important both in the international arena and in the control which it exercised over the political conscience of millions of Frenchmen. Early indicators were not promising. The hierarchy of the 1780s was closely linked both to the ideology of absolutism and to the interests of the nobility; the majority of French bishops and abbots were younger sons of noble families. The Revolution's opposition to privilege, its avowed aim to abolish feudal dues and tithes, and its early concessions to non-Catholics all served to make the Church uncomfortable, with some of the leading clergy joining the early emigration. The Revolution might be treading carefully – just how carefully was demonstrated in 1790 when the people of the papal state of Avignon asked to be annexed to France – but between the Catholic hierarchy and a rationalist ideology compromise would never sit easily. The Papacy made no secret of its dislike for the new government in France, or of the importance which it attached to its alliance with the monarchies of Catholic Europe.

Among the revolutionaries themselves, moreover, fissures were beginning to appear. If all agreed about the primacy of the Rights of Man, there was no agreement about the role which the King should play, nor about the meaning of political liberty. In Paris power increasingly passed to the more radical Patriot Party, which in turn drove the *monarchiens* into opposition. Politics was becoming more ideological, and as such risked becoming more exclusive. In the provinces, too, any early consensus was soon lost as factions fought each other for political control, leaving a legacy of bitterness during the years that followed. And the whole question of political representation remained to be resolved. The nation might be sovereign, but who constituted the nation? Should elections be restricted to the propertied classes and to taxpayers? How, in other words, was the political nation to be defined? In 1789 the deputies gave little thought to ideas of universal suffrage; their goal was to maintain the new political order and to guarantee stable institutions, and memories of the Bastille suggested strongly that the people could be a dangerously anarchic force. In October the Constituent Assembly decreed that political rights would be restricted to active citizens – defined as men over the age of twenty-five who paid the equivalent in taxes of three days' unskilled labour. These were the people, estimated to number around 4.3 million, who were given the right to participate in the electoral process. But that process, as enshrined in the constitution of 1791, was indirect: all that active citizens could do was to choose electors from among their number, and to be an elector one had to pay the equivalent of ten days' labour in tax. Only around fifty thousand men passed this test, which resulted in an electorate considerably more restrictive than that for the elections to the Estates-General in 1789. For the mass of the people few political rights were envisaged; the Assembly even sought to reduce the powers of petitioning, while in Paris the National Guard was given a strong policing role to make the city obedient to the legally constituted authorities. A new political class was being born.

But for how long could distinctions of this sort continue to be justified? Already the Paris popular movement had made its influence felt, and radicals knew that they could hope to call upon it again if the need should arise. A number of journalists and politicians were beginning to take up their cause, to talk of a wider suffrage, of the need for popular sovereignty, even of the right to insurrection. They expressed fears that a limited franchise would lead to tyranny and corruption. Pierre-Jean Audouin argued in the *Journal Universel* that it was the citizens who constituted the nation, and that it was therefore the citizens who had the right to make all the laws of the nation – civil and criminal law, and even those affecting the Church and the military (Censer, 1976, p. 60). Camille Desmoulins, in his *Révolutions de France et de Brabant*, questioned the legal basis of any distinction that divided the citizens against one another: 'But what is this much repeated word *active citizen* supposed to mean? The active citizens are the ones who took the Bastille' (Doyle, 1989, p. 124). The early show of consensus had not lasted long. It is tempting, indeed, to conclude that it had been something of an illusion, an appearance of unity engendered by the passion and euphoria which the summoning of the Estates-General and the formation of the National Assembly had themselves created. That illusion would soon be cruelly shattered as memories of 4 August dimmed and vital practical decisions had to be taken. There remained, of course, wide areas of agreement. All, or almost all, wanted to seize the opportunity which the collapse of the *ancien régime* seemed to present them. No one wanted to reduce France to anarchy. But there agreement ended, for conservatives and radicals had very different ideas about the sort of political and social order they sought to create.

3

Politics

In the eyes of contemporaries the very idea of revolution implied disorder, and disorder on a massive scale. For what was revolution but the deliberate destruction of the values and institutions which underpinned government and gave society its cohesion? Eighteenth-century France was well familiar with the word, which was used to describe a sudden and violent transformation of society, the victory of the new and unpredictable over tried and tested structures. The term had its origins in astronomy and in the discussion of nature, but it was its political application that was most widely discussed. Traditionalists used the word in a pejorative sense, as something to be feared, something which disrupted the stability that governments properly sought to impose on their subjects. Indeed, the traditional definition of 'revolution', to be found in the great dictionaries of the late seventeenth and early eighteenth centuries, emphasized its capacity for destruction virtually to the exclusion of all other aspects. In 1680, for instance, Richelet had defined it with somewhat hostile economy as 'trouble, disorder and change'. In its turn the *Dictionnaire de Trévoux*, in a tone reflecting the views and prejudices of its readers, had linked it to the more negative transformations which threatened mankind, to periods of 'disgrace, misfortune and decadence' (Lucas, 1988, p. 42). It was only with the spread of new ideas during the Enlightenment that the discussion of revolution become more even handed, and only in the last fifty years of the *ancien régime* that political commentators had begun to suggest that it might have a capacity for beneficial change and for the extension of human liberty. Until then there was no place for popular opinion. Political representation was seen as something that necessarily emanated from above; in Keith Baker's phrase, 'the traditional logic of representation under the Old Regime derives from the essential relationship between royal sovereignty and particularistic social order' (Baker, 1987, p. 471). What was permitted from below was deputation.

With the Enlightenment traditional assumptions about the nature of order had come to be challenged, in both the political and the social spheres. It was no longer universally accepted that political stability must necessarily depend upon obedience to an absolute King, who in turn acted as God's representative in his kingdom. Nor was it so obvious that man's principal mission was to serve God, or that his acceptance of the existing order was the only means whereby he could be saved from his own natural sin. Those philosophers, like Voltaire, Mably, or d'Holbach, who questioned the status quo and rejected the idea of a necessary politico-ecclesiastical order in society, were not arguing for anarchy or for political disorder. They believed in another kind of order, an order which placed man more clearly at the centre of the political universe. Existing institutions had to be questioned and if necessary replaced. Rousseau argued that government should reflect a social contract between ruler and ruled and talked of government as a reflection of the 'general will'. Montesquieu advocated a political order which would reflect the diverse interests in society and would guarantee the division of powers; he argued that liberty was best served by the rule of law. Both believed, in contrasting ways, that there had to be a revolutionary change in perceptions of power and in the nature of political order in France. Their ideas, combined with the example of successful revolutionary movements in other countries – in England in the seventeenth century, Geneva in the 1760s, and most recently in the

American colonies in 1776 – helped to give the concept of revolution a new and less damaging public image. The idea of a revolution in France no longer seemed so menacing.

Of course such ideas did not spread indiscriminately through society. In country areas few would have been aware of them; Paris was altogether more receptive. Among artisans and journeymen in the capital, recent research suggests that concepts of natural law and natural justice were understood some decades before 1789 and much used in trade disputes before the Châtelet court (Sonenscher, 1989, pp. 73–98). Here the idea of political insurrection in defence of these rights might be expected to win a wider adherence. And in 1789 itself the level of awareness would greatly increase with the flurry of pamphleteering that heralded the meeting of the Estates-General at Versailles. Not that the initial experience of revolution, when it finally came, was entirely reassuring. Press freedoms were abused, violence went unchecked. Besides, there was no clear agreement as to the purpose of the upheaval they were experiencing. Among the new political class there was no single revolutionary movement, no clear blueprint for the remodelling of government and society. Between 1789 and 1795 France would have a series of contrasting constitutions, each promising a very different kind of system. Executive and judicial functions would be continually redefined, as the system swung from being a limited monarchy to being a republic, and as nationalism and virtue in turn came to inform the polity. There was, it seemed, little consensus, even on such basic matters as individual rights, religious freedoms, citizenship, or the sanctity of property. The country vacillated wildly between devolution and centralized power, between libertarian reform and political terror, between economic liberty and the controls of a war economy. It is arguable, indeed, that between the meeting of the Estates-General in 1789 and the establishment of the Directory in the Year III there was not one single revolution but a succession of revolutions, as different groups in turn attempted to apply their chosen formulae to a nation in flux. Monarchiens and Patriots, Girondins and Montagnards,

Thermidorians and Directorials, each group in turn tried to steer government along paths more suited to its own ideas.

Often they were brought to power by violence, most frequently Parisian violence involving the artisans and workpeople of the capital. We have already seen how the peasant violence of the *Grande Peur* and the popular attack on the Bastille in the summer of 1789 helped to shore up the powers of the National Assembly and push the privileged orders towards compromise. Those who could not contemplate compromise were permitted – some might say encouraged – to leave; the summer of 1789 also saw the first significant emigration by nobles and clergy unable to stomach the changes which they saw around them. But once these early gains had been achieved and the authority of the nation ceased to be challenged the violence did not stop; nor did groups within the political class seek to stop it. Throughout the 1790s crowd violence would remain a crucial element in the French Revolution, a force to be invoked in moments of political crisis. And on each occasion when the people became involved, their intervention seemed to have dramatic consequences. The popular insurrection at the Tuileries in August 1792, with its killing and its martyrs, turned opinion against Louis XVI and his Swiss Guards. The suspension of the King and the declaration of the republic followed. In the summer of 1793 the rising of the Paris sections helped the Jacobins to overthrow the Girondin administration and establish themselves in power. It was to the more radical of the sectional assemblies that they looked for legitimation, especially as they built their siege economy and introduced measures of political terror. But by the spring of 1794 the Jacobins themselves had come to fear the influence of the sections and had distanced themselves from their more extreme egalitarian ideas. Finally, on 9 *thermidor* (27 July 1794), they were in their turn overthrown. Thermidor was essentially a palace revolution within the Assembly, organized by an alliance of moderate republicans, disillusioned Jacobins, and deputies fearful for their own survival. But it owed its success to the fact that the Paris popular movement had become disenchanted with their mode of government and allowed them to fall.

In the months that followed the Thermidorians made sure that they would not be caught in the same trap. They progressively disarmed the Paris crowd and removed the powers of its leaders. Under the Directory the sections were reduced to a pale shadow of their former selves, deprived of the rights and privileges which had ensured their influence in the heady days of the Jacobin republic. Denied the right to sit permanently, refused attendance money and limited to routine bureaucratic functions like the issue of bread cards, they ceased to have any independent political role. They became little more than low-level administrators, carrying out such chores as the government chose to allocate to them. In the process they lost much of their old authority, their ability to galvanize support in the workshops and markets of the capital. By 1795 their impotence was clear; Germinal and Prairial represented the last flickers of a dying political movement. Babeuf's conspiracy in 1796, though able to spark some enthusiasm among the more egalitarian *sectionnaires*, was quickly and efficiently purged. The popular movement as an independent force had ceased to exist. Even then the threat of violence was not removed: these were years of royalist threats and theatre mobs, of *muscadins* and the *jeunesse dorée*, years that culminated in the royalist violence of Prairial (Gendron, 1979, pp. 325–7). Popular Paris, with its long tradition of insurrection, was still treated with deep suspicion by those in government, and was policed with particular rigour in consequence. In the end, of course, the real threat would come not from Paris but from the army. At Brumaire the Directory would be overthrown by a military coup d'état.

Fear of Disorder

In these circumstances it was easy for those opposed to the Revolution to portray it as a slide towards political anarchy.

Some were convinced from the outset that the destruction of the institutions of the *ancien régime* could only lead to disorder; others saw the involvement of the popular movement as the proof they were looking for that government had lost all authority within the country. Monarchists expressed alarm that stability was being forever destroyed; and those who sought shelter in emigration often justified their actions by the claim that the Revolution threatened to plunge France into anarchy. Louis XVI himself, on the eve of his ill-fated flight to Varennes, identified publicly with this view. As long as he had been able to hope that order and the happiness of the kingdom might result from the activities of the National Assembly, he wrote, he had been prepared to stay in revolutionary Paris; but by the summer of 1791 he could no longer entertain such hopes. He claimed that his decision to emigrate had been prompted by the chaos which he now witnessed on all sides, with 'all powers disregarded, property violated, personal security everywhere endangered, crimes unpunished', in short in a France where 'total anarchy was taking the place of law' (Stewart, 1951, p. 205). Others would argue that his collusion with émigré nobles and foreign monarchs had contributed to this anarchy; certainly his exercise of executive authority had done little to reassure those who doubted his good will. But to many political conservatives Louis's explanation seemed convincing: they shared his view that political stability could not result from the conflicting interests and pressures that characterized the early Revolution.

Anarchy, looting, disorder: throughout the Revolution those opposed to further change would resort to this catechism of denunciation. It was not just the language of counter-revolution. It was a language shared by many within the gamut of revolutionary politics who feared being outmanoeuvred by more radical elements. Initially the charge was used by constitutional monarchists against those advocating a republic, since for them the separation of powers and the maintenance of a powerful executive were preconditions of stability. Soon republicans themselves would fall out over the kind of republic they wanted to see established, and the more moderate republicans took up the cry. By 1793 it was the Paris sections and the Paris Jacobin Club which were increasingly perceived as the chief instigators of disorder. They were the principal advocates of exceptional laws and revolutionary tribunals, the most passionate devotees of terror. In many parts of the provinces Paris itself became associated with anarchy and crowd violence. Birotteau, the deputy for the Pyrénées-orientales, summed up the feelings of many provincial Frenchmen when he warned against the long-standing traditions of anarchy that characterized the capital. Shortly after the Jacobin coup of June 1793 he declared that 'anarchy has set up its throne in Paris; it reigns there by the use of terror; and its aim is to enslave the whole of France.' Many deputies agreed. As recently as 25 May the irascible Isnard, who at that moment was president of the Assembly, had threatened that if the violence and anarchy of the Parisians resulted in any of the deputies being harmed, then 'I tell you, in the name of all France, that Paris would be annihilated.' In response to angry cries from the chamber and to a protest from Marat that he was dishonouring the name of the Convention, Isnard had blundered on, insisting that soon one would be forced to 'search the banks of the Seine to discover whether Paris had ever existed' (Hardman, 1973, p. 67).

The Thermidorians rekindled this image of a republic threatened by anarchy and disorder, and turned it to their own ends. Their purpose, as they saw it, was to restore order to a country where popular violence and excess had made good government impossible and where the role of the elected assembly had been usurped by journalists, by clubs, and by popular sections. They therefore sought to distance themselves from the more radical face of the Jacobin Republic and denounced everything that smacked of anarchy. Disorder was identified with Marat and Hébert, those manipulators of popular fury, but also with those who, like Robespierre, had lived by terror and who had abused the powers invested in them. Terror and ambition were thus personalized and practitioners of terror vilified. In this way the Thermidorians believed that they could unite the great mass of the French people, many of whom had been alienated from politics or forced into hiding. Clubs and sections were closed down, newspapers censored, and a ferocious pamphlet war unleashed against those ex-terrorists who still held public office, the so-called 'Queue de Robespierre'. The trials of Fouquier-Tinville and of Carrier were little more than showtrials. In the departments *livres rouges* denounced local Jacobins and those who had held any form of public office during the Terror. In those parts of the country where family and clan loyalties ran deep, most especially in the south east, purges were once again the order of the day. All this activity, as Bronislaw Baczko has pointed out, had a simple political goal – to exorcise the memory of the Terror and to bring revolutionary upheaval to an end. By these tactics, he argues, they sought to legitimize the Republic (Lucas, 1988, pp. 348–9).

For this reason, if for no other, the propaganda of the post-thermidorian period has to be treated with some suspicion. Besides, the political leadership was largely derived from those who, in 1793 and 1794, had served as deputies on mission to the provinces. Their activity at that time scarcely suggests that they were viscerally opposed to the use of terror: men like Tallien, Fréron or Barras were as ruthless as any of their peers in their repression of the federalist revolts in Bordeaux and the Midi. 'We are killing everything that moves', Fréron had written from Toulon during the repression of the city's revolt (Crook, 1991, p. 150). If some months later he was on the winning side, where is the evidence that his views had been transformed?

There is, of course, a sense in which revolutionaries are dedicated, almost by definition, to a great deal of destruction. The existing administrative and legal structures had to be dismantled, and the assumptions on which they were based rethought. Parlements, estates, ecclesiastical and seigneurial courts, local administrations, all had a rationale that was tightly linked to the old monarchy. Their abolition must therefore be seen as an integral part of the subsequent restructuring of the country's institutional base, as a necessary first step in the creation of a new political order in France. Contemporaries were certainly aware of the need to destroy before they could rebuild. Those who represented the Third Estate at Versailles, who bound themselves by the Tennis Court Oath and who denounced the corporate nature of French society were very conscious that they were liberating their fellow citizens and guaranteeing their new-found freedoms. The new order was to be liberal and pluralist, based on the humanitarian ideals of the Enlightenment, on concepts of citizenship and of civic obligation which found their fullest expression in the Declaration of the Rights of Man. Frenchmen were to be guaranteed the basic freedoms which had been denied them under the Bourbon monarchy – freedom of speech, freedom to trade, freedom to own property. Those with property, those who paid a given amount in taxes, would have rights of citizenship, including the right to vote and the right to stand for political office – property would confer the right to be involved in the political processes of the state. Men would be equal before the law; habeas corpus would be guaranteed; executive abuses would be curtailed. Most importantly, these rights would be consecrated by a constitution, which in turn would bind future generations of lawmakers. Like all liberals the men of 1789 attached great importance to constitution making. A constitution was the mechanism by which they could establish and maintain their liberties. Through it a new political order would be created; and the constitutional choices made in September 1789 ensured that it would be, in Mona Ozouf's words, 'radical and rousseauist' in conception (Furet and Ozouf, 1988, p. 49).

But ideas of liberty were difficult to control, human aspirations difficult to order. In 1789 the *cahiers de doléances* had already raised popular expectations, while economic crises had only served to hasten the demand for change. Conflicting ideologies, popular radicalism, war and counter-revolution would all play their part in distorting and corrupting the original ideals. Many of the early revolutionaries were idealistic reformers who wanted to liberalize the law and to abolish much

of the privilege on which French society was based; they
wanted to force Louis XVI to accept a limited monarchy, to
rule constitutionally rather than as an absolute monarch. They
were content that their work should stop there. But if such
reformers had their place in the France of 1789, their power
and influence were soon challenged by others. In October 1789
Mounier decided that there was no place for him in the alien
world that was coming into being, and sought safety in emigration. Others would follow him. By January 1791 Barnave had
returned home to the Dauphiné. In November the mayor of
Paris, Bailly, the object of Parisian hatred following the mas-
sacre at the Champ de Mars, resigned in disillusionment. And
Lafayette, the one-time hero of two worlds, was being denounced as an adventurer and as a potential dictator long before
he defected to the Austrians. Their place at the centre of
politics was taken by a new generation of politicians, by men
who were younger, often more clinically logical in their judgements, men who had a different, more radical vision of what a
revolutionary political order embraced. This new generation,
men like Jacques-Pierre Brissot and Maximilien Robespierre,
were mostly committed republicans who had little interest in
the maintenance of constitutional monarchy.

France did not have one single political revolution in the
decade that followed 1789, but several. Constitutional monarchy, the panacea advocated by almost all the first generation
of revolutionaries, was unable to recover its credibility after the
King's attempted flight to Varennes in the summer of 1791.
The call for Louis to be deposed and for a republic to be
declared gathered in strength, especially after the declaration of
war on Austria and Prussia. The King and more especially his
Queen, Marie-Antoinette, were widely deemed to be untrustworthy, unpatriotic, in league with the Emperor. The summer
of 1792 saw mass demonstrations in Paris, with national guardsmen from the provinces arriving in the capital to celebrate the
aniversary of the Bastille and joining forces with the more
radical Parisians. On 10 August they attacked the royal palace
at the Tuileries: in the fierce fighting which ensued several

hundred Parisians were killed, and the angry crowd took its revenge by slaughtering around six hundred of the King's Swiss Guards after they had surrendered. The royal family escaped, but its image was badly tarnished; Louis was the King who had used foreign mercenaries to fire on his own people. The Assembly responded by deposing the King, imprisoning the entire royal family, and declaring France a republic. In the eyes of both contemporaries and historians 10 August opened a second, much more fanatical phase of the Revolution.

In December Louis would be put on trial before the new assembly, the National Convention. His defence counsel, the Bordeaux lawyer De Sèze, argued strongly that, as King, Louis had been above the law and that putting him on trial was an act of dubious legality. Though many deputies shared these legal doubts, few were convinced of the innocence of his actions; in particular, it was generally accepted that he had conspired with the Austrians against his own people. It was not the verdict that was in question, but the sentence. What could be done with a king found guilty of treason, in a nation at war, that would not endanger the security of the state? If he were imprisoned he might become a rallying-point for counter-revolution. But if he were executed, would he not be transformed into a martyr, revered by French royalists and foreign monarchs alike? Many deputies held back from regicide, believing that an appeal to the people of France would save Louis's life. Others held that if the Revolution were to be saved, then Louis must die. 'If he is innocent', argued Saint-Just, 'the people are guilty' (Hampson, 1991, p. 87). In the event, of course, the sterner logic prevailed: Louis was condemned to death by the narrowest of margins – 361 deputies voted for death, as against 360 who sought by one means or another to avoid his execution – and on 21 January 1793 he was guillotined on the Place de la Révolution in Paris. A huge crowd roared its approval as the executioner held up the King's head, the most potent symbol that the old order had finally been swept away.

But the key political questions remained to be answered. What sort of republic should France seek to be, with what kind of political institutions? The problems of life without a king proved almost as great as those of life with him. Where did executive power now lie, and what should be the relationship between the executive and the deputies? Should power be extended to those without property; were they, too, entitled to the full rights of citizenship? And where exactly did sovereignty lie? There might be general agreement that it lay in the nation, but what did that mean? Once it had voted for its deputies did the nation retain any rights? Was there any place in politics for clubs and political societies, or for the Paris sections, the radicals whose activism had proved so vital in consolidating early political gains? Did the people have any right to protest or remonstrate against the decisions of the deputies; did they, indeed, retain the right to insurrection? These were fundamental questions which the revolutionaries were unable to avoid once the King had been deposed and the republic declared. Those who had been united in wanting France to become a republic before September 1792 – including men who had been among the most radical deputies of the Legislative Assembly – were now divided over the kind of republic they should devise.

Political divisions

The main political division in 1792 and 1793 was between the Girondins and the Montagnards. But what was it that distinguished them? Both groups, after all, shared similar republican principles; both had belonged to the Jacobin Club; both believed in liberty, equality before the law, and the rights of property. Nor is it possible to draw any clear social distinction between them. The Girondins might be slightly wealthier and have stronger links with the trading and legal elites of the larger provincial cities; but there was no social gulf between them and their Montagnard opponents. Alison Patrick notes that the Girondins were archetypal provincial *notables*, strongly represented in the trading ports and along the Atlantic coastline, and with some strength in conservative areas (like the Somme) where the danger of counter-revolution was slight. Their successes were more concentrated than those of the Montagne – 40 per cent of their deputation came from only eleven departments – and, crucially, they had no representation in Paris (Patrick, 1972, pp. 190–3). Their leaders, too, came from the provinces: Roland, for instance, was identified with Lyon, and Vergniaud, Guadet, and Gensonné – that cluster of orators who represented the Gironde and gave the group their name – with Bordeaux. Their ideas were both economically and politically liberal: many of them had identified with Brissot over the slaving issue and the Amis des Noirs or had joined Nicolas de Bonneville in his liberal publishing house, the Cercle Social (Kates, 1985, pp. 6–8). Already the Girondins had formed a short-lived ministry during the Legislative Assembly, and they had spoken out strongly in favour of war, which Robespierre and the leading Montagnards opposed. And already their conduct of affairs was being severely censured by Robespierre – not just their advocacy of war, but also their close association with General Dumouriez, who in March 1793 denounced French policy and followed Lafayette's example by going across to the Austrians. Girondin ministers, it was implied, were impetuous, untrustworthy, and associated with traitors. Above all, in Montagnard eyes, they were guilty of the most serious sin of all: they were anti-Parisian, distrustful of the capital and always ready to denounce the excesses of the popular movement.

If the Girondins can only be defined in a loose and descriptive way, the same is true of their opponents. For though the Montagnards observed tighter group unity, largely by rehearsing their arguments at the Jacobin Club, the difference was one of degree. Indeed it would be difficult to divide the Convention with any assurance into Girondins and Montagnards; deputies voted as individuals on many issues, and there were some two hundred and fifty members, known collectively as the Plain, who belonged to neither group, maintaining a degree of aloofness from what they regarded as factional politics. The committed Montagnards can, however, be easily identified. They came largely from the radical wing of the Jacobins after the Club had split into moderate and radical factions, with Lameth, Barnave and the more conservative among them taking the name of Feuillants. And they maintained their loyalty to the Jacobins. From 1793, when the Paris Club was purged of moderates, the identification of Jacobins and Montagnards would become almost total, to the point where politicians like Robespierre, Danton, and Marat gloried in both descriptions. Their geographical base was also very different from that of the Gironde. Though represented in most parts of provincial France – including much of the south west outside the immediate catchment of Bordeaux – they were also strongly implanted in Paris. Indeed, in the elections to the Convention in September 1792 the capital did not return a single Girondin deputy, which effectively made the Montagnards the group that represented Paris and Parisian interests. In the months that followed there would be close liaison between Montagnard leaders, the Paris Commune and the radical sections, which in turn fuelled Girondin fears of renewed popular violence. It was only too easy to portray the Jacobins as demagogues, men dependent on the approval of the Commune, who defended the popular movement because they might at any time need to call on it to maintain themselves in power.

When the National Convention assembled on 21 September the battle between the Gironde and the Montagne was the dominant feature of republican politics. Though no group enjoyed a majority – and the notion of 'party' is still highly anachronistic – the Girondins were able to form their second ministry, and almost immediately they were sucked into a bitter quarrel over Paris. This was at a moment when the capital had been swept by panic, induced by news of the fall of Longwy and the fear of an enemy assault on the city. Incited by the rhetoric of Marat, the Commune and its agents had, between 2 and 7 September, coordinated attacks on the city's prisons, where the crowd had invaded the cells, dragging out priests and supposed aristocrats, and hacking over 1,100 victims to death (Lewis, 1993, p. 38). The September Massacres were the most grisly single incident in the Revolution, an example of lynch law and of a crowd baying for blood. But the fact that the Girondins condemned them and demanded that the perpetrators be brought to justice led the Montagnards to defend the Parisians against the government, even if few Montagnard leaders actually condoned what had happened. The damage, however, was done: the Girondins were designated as moderates, defenders of property, enemies of Paris and its popular sections. In contrast, the Montagnards presented themselves as men of principle whose republicanism retained a place for popular politics. In the months that followed the September Massacres these divisions grew deeper. Over the King's trial the Montagne were united in demanding the death penalty; the Girondins showed their fatal individualism and indecision in voting at cross-purposes, putting their faith in an appeal to the people in the hope that the people would pull back from killing their king. Their inability to work consistently as a group or to accept that individuality had sometimes to be subsumed proved an insuperable weakness. Defeats in the war and counter-revolution in the west further undermined their authority in government. By the summer of 1793 the Montagnards were ready to stage their own revolution. On 29 May Robespierre made his move at the Paris Jacobins; the Paris sections responded, and between 31 May and 2 June the Convention was invaded and the Girondin leaders arrested.

Within a ten-month period, therefore, France witnessed two major changes in political control which transformed the character of the Revolution itself. First the country became a republic; then it passed under the control of the Montagne. Yet again the deputies were faced with the task of providing the country with a constitution, since that of 1791 had already outlived its usefulness, dying along with the Bourbon monarchy in August 1792. The decision was made to confer executive and legislative power to a single body, the Convention, but it was left to the newly elected deputies to draw up a republican constitution that France required. There was, once again, no easy agreement on the form such a constitution should take, with both the Girondins and the Montagnards drawing up their separate proposals. The Girondin one was destined to remain a piece of paper; that of the Jacobins was ratified by national vote in June 1793. It got rid at a stroke of many of the earlier checks and balances between Paris and the provinces. Legislative and executive authority were concentrated in the Convention, while sovereignty lay unequivocally with the people. The insistence on decentralization which had so exercised the deputies in 1789 was quietly forgotten. Among the rights of man now held out to the French people were the right to public assistance and to state education, and the right to resist oppression by insurrection (Doyle, 1989, p. 244). And all adult males were now to have full rights of citizenship, not just a propertied minority. In electoral terms this represented a huge widening of the suffrage compared to that enshrined in the constitution of 1791. Then the percentage of active citizens had varied markedly between regions of the country, with rural areas generally more democratic than urban centres. In Paris, for instance, only around 9.5 per cent of men had had the right to vote, whereas in a sparsely populated department like the Basses-Alpes the figure rose to 19.4 per cent. Now even those foreigners resident in France who were adjudged to have performed notable services in the cause of humanity were to be allowed the vote. It was a generous constitution, favouring the legislature over the executive, and prescribing annual elections and direct voting to try to ensure that government would remain answerable to the people of France.

Yet theory and practice were to prove very different. The constitution of 1793 was ratified, and on 10 August – the anniversary of the deposition of the King – it was officially promulgated. But it was never put into effect. On the next day, when it was proposed that the Convention should dissolve itself to make way for constitutional government, Robespierre violently opposed the idea as playing into the hands of France's enemies and hampering the country's war effort. The Convention remained, and the powers of its executive committees were greatly strengthened. Hence the liberties which the constitution promised were never enjoyed, the annual elections never held. On 10 October, following Saint-Just's report on revolutionary government – 'it is impossible for revolutionary laws to be enacted as long as the government itself is not constituted in a revolutionary manner' – emergency powers were introduced that were to last until peace was signed (Hardman, 1973, p. 157). Even Robespierre, once the staunchest advocate of the Montagnard constitution, now spoke in favour of its suspension. On 25 December he warned critics of revolutionary government that they should not hide behind constitutional arguments, for, he implied, France in her present condition could not afford the luxury of constitutionalism. 'The object of a revolutionary regime is to found a republic, that of a constitutional regime is to carry it on. The first befits a time of war between liberty and its enemies; the second suits a time when freedom is victorious, and at peace with the world' (Thompson, 1935, p. 438).

The constitution of 1793 would never be put into effect, since the Montagnards were overthrown on 9 *thermidor* (27 July 1794) and the Thermidorians had little liking for its broad suffrage and democratic vision. And just as they cut the influence of the Paris popular movement, deeming it a force for violence and disorder, so they sought to establish a constitution that would better reflect propertied interests and thus ensure what they saw as greater governmental responsibility. The outcome was the constitution of the Year III, which introduced France's first bicameral legislature, operated by a system of indirect elections. There were to be two chambers – the Conseil des Cinq-Cents and the Conseil des Anciens – and to vote, a man had to be a French citizen, to be over twenty-one years of age, to pay direct taxes and to be resident for at least a year in his canton. As for executive power, it was to reside in a Directory of five members nominated by the legislature in its capacity as an electoral assembly speaking in the name of the nation. The separation of the executive from the legislature was intended to give the executive a greater measure of independence, and the new constitution marked a significant move

away from democratic answerability and towards a more conservative interpretation of political order. It was a trend which
would become even more marked following the coup of 18
brumaire and the coming to power of Napoleon Bonaparte (Cole
and Campbell, 1989, pp. 35–42).

Many would see this concentration of power as a logical
product of the entire revolutionary period, since from the very
outset the Revolution had sought to create a national political
order, with legal decisions made at the centre and applied
equally across the country. Local differences and regional
traditions were not only discouraged; they were seen as being
dangerous and potentially counter-revolutionary, remnants of
an *ancien régime* where provincial power was the prerogative of
the nobility. Hence the bias of the Revolution was towards
finding a national legislative solution to every problem. Laws
passed in Paris had to be implemented throughout the country;
all trace of local legal codes or of seigneurial and clerical
jurisdictions had to be erased. Equality – 'la sainte égalité' so
beloved of revolutionary speech writers – demanded that this
be so, that the fruits of the Revolution be equally available to
all. But this in turn implied a huge volume of legislation and
the demolition of old, time-honoured practices. It demanded a
revolution in methods of administration and policing, new
courts and tribunals, a vast extension of the traditional role of
the state in the lives of the people. And if it was to be
successful, it required changes of an even more fundamental
kind – changes in habit and outlook on the part of ordinary
Frenchmen, an acceptance of their new national identity and of
the full implications of citizenship.

Implementing the new political order

The new political order had to permeate down into local
communities if it were to make a serious impression on the
habits of centuries. One of the first tasks of the constitutional
committee was therefore to examine the existing divisions of

the country and to suggest what it saw as necessary processes of rationalization. To carry out this work it established a special Comité de Division, concerned to redraw the administrative map of France. In his report to the National Assembly on 29 September 1789, the chairman of the committee, Thouret, argued that the existing structure was haphazard and illogical, with too many overlapping jurisdictions. There was no necessary relationship between the units of ecclesiastical administration (*diocèses*), royal administration (*généralités*), military administration (*gouvernements*), and judicial administration (*bailliages*). These conflicting authorities, he believed, were harmful as well as illogical, an impediment to efficiency and an affront to equality. They encouraged waste and led to endless confusion. And often they took no account of public access. Peasants could find themselves denied the justice to which they were entitled because rivers were in spate or snow blocked mountain passes. Provincial boundaries, argued Thouret, should be respected wherever possible in any new administrative division of France, but geographical features, distances and the convenience of those administered should be paramount considerations (Ozouf-Marignier, 1989, pp. 39–42).

The structure which he proposed for local government was based upon a new unit of administration, the department. In the eyes of the deputies who formed the Comité de Division, it was both rational and beneficial for the people of France to abolish the old provincial divisions, and to replace them with 'between seventy-five and eighty-five' departmental units which would be approximately equal in population and in territory and would thus allow an equality of access to administration and to law. Besides, the change had ideological implications: it was a very public statement of the symbolic destruction of monarchy and privilege – for it was not just the provinces that were abolished, but the intendants, the parlements, the whole panoply of *ancien régime* administration. With the Civil Constitution of the Clergy in 1790 the old episcopal sees would also be scrapped, and Church administration inserted into the same departmental structure. The Church, too,

Figure 2 The departments of France in 1790
Source: D. M. G. Sutherland, *France, 1789–1815: Revolution and Counter-Revolution (Collins, 1985).*

would be compelled to reform itself in accordance with the dictates of reason. In practice, of course, tradition was not abandoned overnight. Despite the Assembly's reluctance to admit that the old provinces had any inherent advantages, most departments were sub-divisions of provinces or followed former provincial boundaries. And where a town could show that it had played an administrative role in the life of the surrounding countryside, that, rather than its commercial achievement or crude calculations based on the *cadastre*, generally ensured that it would become departmental *chef-lieu*.

The process of *découpage* was as complex as it was ambitious, a process whose avowed aim was to bring government into closer contact with the people and to give the people more equal access to the courts. It was not just the division into departments that was carried out in 1790, but the further division into districts and cantons, and the placement of tribunals, justices of the peace, schools and colleges. Local opinion was extensively lobbied and interests consulted: Paris was in no position to impose a new administrative map on France without considerable local help. Local politicians and power-brokers tried to ensure that their local communities were protected or rewarded in the ensuing carve-up: the Department of the Hautes-Pyrénées, for example, almost certainly owed its existence to the power and influence of that great manipulator, Bertrand Barère (Laffon and Soulet, 1982, p. 186). This in turn gave rise to endless rows and to bitter acrimony between rival communities, acrimony which often continued to colour their relations throughout ten years of revolution. For the administrative revolution inevitably produced losers as well as winners. A town which lost the prestige or the economic advantage of a tribunal or a seat of administration might continue to plot and to petition in 1793 and 1794, sometimes pointing to the political mistakes of its successful rival in an effort to convince the Convention of its worthiness for consideration. It might even be so angered by the imagined slight as to be tempted by counter-revolution or by the siren voices of federalism.

The departmental system was not perfect, but the new administrative habits quickly took root. Taxation, education, policing, requisitions, recruitment – all were discussed and organized by the new departmental authorities. They were also a valuable vector of opinion and propaganda for the government in the provinces. Through the mayors of some forty thousand communes laws and decrees could be taken into the smallest villages in the farthest corners of the land. Even Napoleon saw no reason to reverse the work of the Comité de Division in matters of local government. He did not wish to revive the institutions that had been destroyed in 1789, noting rather the 'chaos of the provincial assemblies' and the 'pretensions of the parlements' that had characterized the old system. France, he said, had been more a collection of twenty kingdoms than a single state, and he had no desire to return to the abuses which such a system implied. Those changes which he did make sought to strengthen the departments, not, it is true, as agents of local opinion, but as units of administration that helped forge France into a single governable whole. In particular, he introduced the prefects as agents of central authority in the departments, men appointed from the centre who might take advice from local people but whose sole loyalty was to the state through the Minister of the Interior. To Napoleon the French people were no longer 'citoyens' – and the change of language is not without its significance; they were 'administrés', cogs in an efficient system of administration. And the reforms which the Revolution had introduced in the name of devolution would be an important element in the realization of the Napoleonic dream.

There is no real contradiction here. The Revolution had championed more devolved authority in its early stages largely in reaction to the system of royal intendants, which it too easily mistook for tyranny. Devolution from the centre was undoubtedly popular at a time when criticisms of the *ancien régime* focused on ministerial despotism and abuses of royal authority. During the municipal revolution of 1789–90 new powers were given to mayors and town councils, and these councils were themselves answerable to their constituents through elections. But this does not mean that it was the government's intention to loosen the reins of political control. If power became decentralized, it was mostly because administrative structures were still in their infancy and communication between local bodies was still poor. Even in 1790 the system had considerable internal logic, considerable potential for integration. The will to control was already present.

As the Revolution faced greater and greater crises – food supplies, military movements, counter-revolution and royalism – so the need for control became more obvious. The war, as we have seen, posed a particular problem of public safety. The *patrie* was declared to be *en danger*, and exceptional measures of government were authorized. Under the Jacobin Republic of 1793–4 local powers were largely abolished with the institution of 'revolutionary government', and terror was declared the order of the day. Control and obedience were increasingly emphasized and any deviations from national policy ruthlessly punished. Local initiatives, indeed, came to be treated with distrust. In the process a whole new network of officialdom was put in place. Deputies were sent out on mission from the Convention to enforce the law and to educate local administrators, and when they became suspected of showing too much independence – mostly in the spring and summer of 1794 – they might be recalled to Paris or subjected to surveillance and investigation. To ensure that the new revolutionary laws were enforced and that suspects were brought to trial, *agents nationaux*, answerable to the Minister of the Interior, replaced locally answerable public prosecutors. Local officials were ordered to report back to Paris every ten days outlining the problems they faced. At every level there was a call for surveillance and accountability; the suspicion was always present that local functionaries did not share the ideals of the Jacobins, that they were lax in their administration and lukewarm in their political commitment. Revolutionary committees were to be established in every commune to supervise public order and to denounce the failings of administrators. Radical militants were organized as battalions of the *armée révolution-naire* to arrest suspects and to ensure that grain convoys reached the cities and the military. The political order established at the centre had to be extended to every commune in France.

Revolutionary government as it was decreed by the Montagnards had no place for pluralism and made no allowance for political disagreement. The law of 14 *frimaire* II made this abundantly clear: the Convention, it specified, was where all initiative belonged. And for the Convention one could increasingly read the tightly knit executive committees within the Convention where the inner circle of Montagnards exercised power – most particularly, of course, the Committee of Public Safety, which was concerned with all matters of internal order and policing. From here would come the torrent of legislation which sought to regenerate France and to inculcate a new system of political values. These were also the months when the personal power of Robespierre was being extended into virtually every aspect of governmental activity. Contemporaries were well aware of this, and often they noted it with alarm. Even among his closer associates in the Jacobin Club there were many who feared Robespierre's aspirations to dictatorship and the distortion of the ideals in which they believed. In 1794 the egalitarian Gracchus Babeuf was to comment that 'there are two Robespierres, the one a genuine *patriote* and man of principle, up to the 31st of May [1793], and since then the man of ambition, the tyrant and the deepest of villains' (Hampson, 1974, p. viii). Robespierre himself insisted that it was the pursuit of virtue, more even than the immediate dangers which threatened France, that justified emergency powers and the resort to terror. In Saint-Just's phrase, 'the only function of law is to repel evil; innocence and virtue go their ways about the earth freely' (Hampson, 1981, p. 17). The unvirtuous come to be regarded as a dangerous cancer within the body politic which had to be excised if the republic were to survive.

Terror

Terror must be seen as more than an emergency response to a crisis situation, more than a series of exceptional laws aimed at rooting out the political crimes which threatened the security of the state. Rather it was an integral part of the government process, closely tied in with policies of administrative centralization. From the passing of the Law of Suspects in September 1793 until the fall of the Jacobins ten months later the government moved farther and farther away from the liberal ideals of the early revolution, farther down the road towards a police state. Basic civil rights like habeas corpus and trial by jury – granted only recently and still in force for ordinary criminal charges – were withdrawn in cases where the security of the state was thought to be at risk. Under the terms of the most extreme of terrorist measures, the Law of 22 *Prairial* II (10 June 1794), the calling of witnesses was left to the discretion of the court and the accused was denied the aid of defence counsel; and, where the defendant was found guilty, the only sentence available was death. This law ushered in a second and far more terrible phase of terror during the spring and summer of 1794, when whole batches of suspects were condemned and sent to their deaths on the Place de la Révolution. The vast majority were political suspects; few were executed for economic crimes. Indeed, it is significant that measures of economic terror – like the Ventôse Decrees of February and March 1794, ordering that the goods of those 'recognised as the enemies of the revolution' should be sequestered – were scarcely implemented (Doyle, 1989, p. 266). In all Donald Greer estimates that around half a million Frenchmen were imprisoned or placed under house arrest during the months of the Terror; perhaps 16,500 died on the scaffold. When those who died in prison or while awaiting trial are added to this figure, the number of deaths rises to over thirty thousand (Greer, 1935, pp. 25–37). For many Jacobins there was little in these figures to shock. They preferred to see terror as a vital means of purging the country of those who, by their acts and

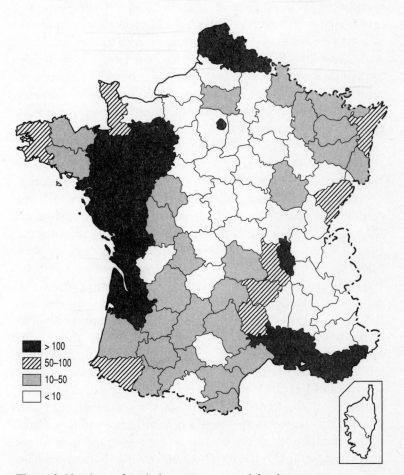

Figure 3 Numbers of capital sentences passed, by department
Source: D. Greer, *The Incidence of the Terror during the French Revolution*
(Harvard University Press, 1935).

opinions, had already excluded themselves from the nation and hence from the enjoyment of any rights of citizenship.

And yet there were many ways in which revolutionary government remained a crisis measure, born out of desperation and from the culture of fear which the Revolution had itself helped to breed. It changed in character over time, as the paranoia of those in power grew more acute, their fear of their rivals more consuming. In the autumn of 1793 Robespierre was still prepared to intervene against the excessive use of violence, saving the lives of seventy-five deputies who had sympathized with the Girondins in June and had signed a secret protest against their purge. Between October and the end of December, despite the emergency legislation, only 177 people were executed in Paris. But in Lyon, Marseille and Bordeaux there were hundreds of executions in the wake of the federalist revolts in these cities; by April 1794, in Lyon alone, over 1,800 death sentences would be carried out (Doyle, 1989, p. 154). And in Paris, too, the spring of 1794 would see terrorist legislation turned against political opponents rather than aristocrats and counter-revolutionaries. Robespierre, in particular, used terror to protect his own increasingly isolated position, ordering the trial of those whom he saw as extremists or rivals to his own brand of Jacobin centralism. The decision to execute the Girondin leaders in the wake of the Jacobin coup set a dangerous precedent that politicians who found themselves on the losing side could expect no mercy. By the spring of 1794 terror was being used against rivals within the Jacobin movement and against leaders of the Paris *sans-culottes*. Right and left were equally at risk. On 13 March the committees ordered the arrest of Hébert, Vincent, Ronsin and sixteen of their fellow militants on the Paris Commune; they were condemned and executed on trumped-up charges of aspiring to military dictatorship and being enemy agents in time of war. Soon afterwards, it was the turn of those involved in the East India Company scandal, to whom were added Danton, Camille Desmoulins and leading moderate critics of the government from within the Jacobin movement. Again, though it would not have been difficult to make convincing charges of corruption, the accusations were vague and entirely political in character. This was especially true in the case of Danton, whose oratorical skills and personal popularity made him a danger to Robespierre. As Norman Hampson puts it, 'the accusation amounted to the charge that Danton's whole career had been one of personal ambition that required monarchy for its satisfaction' (Hampson 1978, p. 169). Danton defended himself with eloquence and dignity, but again the outcome was predetermined, as he well understood. 'I have said it already and I repeat: my domicile will soon be in oblivion and my name in the Pantheon. ... Here is my head to answer for everything.... Life is a burden to me. I am impatient to be rid of it.' In the short term Robespierre's position might seem secured; but deputies became more and more alarmed for their own safety. In Hampson's phrase, the Terror was becoming its own executioner (Hampson, 1981, p. 27).

Terrorist laws might in principle extend over the whole country, but in practice they were unevenly applied, often in response to local circumstances. Food shortages or riots could attract the attention of Paris or evoke the interest of a deputy on mission; refractory priests might stir local passions and antagonize urban officials; looting, desertion and low morale could bring the guillotine into the armies. The circumstances of the Terror could be so terribly arbitrary, with repression the consequence of personal whim or jealousy. It is true that special tribunals were established in towns and regions which were seen as kernels of political opposition, like Lyon and Bordeaux, Nantes and Rochefort. And the six departments of the west, the *Vendée militaire*, suffered a predictable blood-letting. But elsewhere chance played a major part. Much depended on the character of the deputies on mission sent to a department; whereas some sought to understand the problems of local people and took full account of their ignorance or isolation, others – like Joseph Le Bon in the north – went far beyond the letter of the law in imposing terror and seeking out victims for the guillotine (Gobry, 1991, p. 69). In some cases, as with

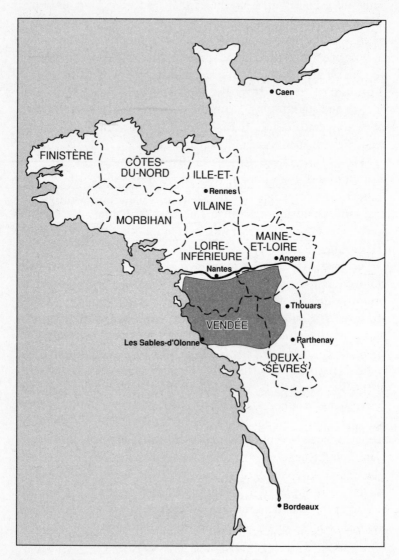

Figure 4 The risings in the west: the *Vendée Militaire*
Source: P. M. Jones, *The Peasantry in the French Revolution* (Cambridge University Press, 1988).

Claude Javogues in the Loire, personal hatreds mingled easily with a desire to settle old scores, as he turned the Terror against the relatively well-off farmers of the Forez and against the pernicious influence of priests; for, he believed, fanaticism was inherently counter-revolutionary, 'sold to the cause of the rich and of kings' (Lucas, 1973, p. 90). All responsibility, however, cannot be laid at the door of deputies sent down from Paris. Many of the most bloodthirsty were local men, whose intolerance reflected that of their own communities. And in regions like the south east, where there was brutal and bloody terror, convictions depended on the evidence of local people, on the denunciations and counter-denunciaØ/ Æ village communities. Elsewhere there were fewer denunciations; local people did not break rank. Or there were fewer perceived problems of supply to alert Paris to possible dissension. In seven departments – the Aube, Basses-Alpes, Hautes-Alpes, Haute-Saône, Seine-et-Marne, and the two Corsican departments – not a single death sentence was handed down; in thirty-one others there were fewer than ten. In contrast, nearly a fifth of all executions took place in a single department, the Maine-et-Loire. The majority of those condemned were working men, artisans and peasants captured bearing arms against the Republic, to whom little mercy was ever accorded (Greer, 1935, pp. 161–4).

The implementation of these measures could not be achieved overnight. Revolutionary government depended ultimately on the enthusiasm of militants, on the fact that there were many men, principally clubists and sectional radicals, who were happy to supervise the conduct of others, to round up suspects, to help impose the new political order. They were crucial to the workings of Revolutionary government, which remained ill equipped to administer such ambitious goals. For France was not a modern society with a modern bureaucratic machine: there were no professional civil servants and very few policemen who could ensure that the stream of laws and decrees emanating from Paris evoked some kind of respect in the country at large. It was not until the later part of the decade, the years of the Directory, that the government made substantial progress in the creation of a modern civil service – men who saw themselves as administrators rather than as political activists, men who could be depended upon to carry out the wishes of whatever government was in power (Church, 1981, p. 111). Nor did the Revolution have at its disposal the force with which to compel a surly or refractory population to obey the law. In the countryside, especially, policing was woefully primitive. The police force they recruited – the gendarmes who took over from the old *maréchaussée* – were little more efficient than the men they replaced. They were desperately short staffed and were generally recruited from among army veterans who had already fulfilled their military obligations to the state. Morale was low, pay derisory, and literacy levels poor. Gendarmes did little more than patrol highways, police markets, and hunt for deserters; and in times of national peril they risked being removed from their policing duties to supplement the troops on the frontier. In short, the Revolution had neither the administrative nor the coercive capacity to enforce its laws: hence its reliance on local Jacobins and on units of the *armée révolutionnaire* (Cobb, 1987). It had to rely on militancy and enthusiasm as a means of effecting its policies.

Propaganda

What they lacked in coercive power the Jacobins sought to achieve by persuasion and propaganda. The message of the Revolution, with its slogans and captions, its stress on citizenship and celebration of fraternity, was a powerful agent of politicization, especially among the urban masses. It was a message that could be put across in many different forms, many of them intruding subtly into the commonplaces of day-to-day life. Reminders of their political identity appeared all around them – in pamphlets and popular papers, in songs and chants, in clothing and cockades, in patriotic festivals. In the armies of the Republic watchwords and uniforms all carried a clear political message, while the Minister of War distributed Hébert's *Père Duchesne* for the instruction of the troops. With civilians the state lacked the same capacity to coerce, but the revolutionary message was everywhere apparent. They might be educated through attendance at clubs and sections (in the summer of 1793 clubs flourished in as many as two thousand towns and villages), by the intense campaign against organized religion, by attendance at patriotic plays in their local theatre. As citizens they wore the red-white-and-blue cockade of the republic in their hats, cheered loudly as symbols of feudalism were chipped away from public buildings, and dutifully used the fraternal 'tu' of the good republican in their daily business. They observed the revolutionary calendar, taking every tenth day off and working on Sundays. They took note of the many name changes to towns and villages, streets and squares, as the names of kings, nobles and saints were removed in a flurry of *débaptisations*. They welcomed, or at least tolerated, the removal or destruction of religious images in the outburst of secularism that accompanied dechristianization. Religious statues were ceremonially toppled and saints chipped away from their traditional niches; around the portals of the great Gothic cathedrals of the Ile-de-France stone saints were solemnly guillotined at the height of the Terror. There were so many different registers in which the citizen could be reminded of his civic duties and dazzled by the sheer effrontery of what had been achieved.

Most notable among these were the numerous popular festivals where ordinary people were brought face to face with the powerful symbolism of the Revolution. At these festivals they lined up alongside mayors and public officials and mingled with soldiers and national guardsmen. They planted trees of liberty, wore the *bonnet rouge*, and swathed themselves in tricolor sashes. Marianne, the female allegory of Liberty, came to symbolize the state: in Maurice Agulhon's words, she became 'a double allegory: she represented both Liberty, an eternal value, and at the same time the newly constituted regime of the

French Republic' (Agulhon, 1981, p. 18). They gloried in
sacrifice and martyrdom – even in the sacrifice of young
children, boys like Bara and Viala who had given their lives
fighting against the enemies of the Republic in the Vendée and
at Avignon. At patriotic festivals they praised the virtues of
childhood or old age, gave thanks for the success of the harvest,
and delighted in the latest French victory. Everything was
heavily imbued with symbolism. In the annual *fêtes de la
Fédération* they dedicated themselves to fraternity and republican unity. And during the Jacobin months they were expected
to take part in festivals of a more blatantly ideological kind,
celebrating the overthrow of organized religion or singing the
praises of the Goddess of Reason. These festivals often assumed the outward trappings of religion, the holidays and
processions with which the Church had marked the passage of
the agricultural year; their reinstatement in secular form represented, in Mona Ozouf's words, a 'transfer of sacrality' to the
revolutionary state (Ozouf, 1988, p. 262). The national guards
who came to Paris to celebrate the taking of the Bastille were,
says James Leith, 'like pilgrims visiting a holy city, birthplace
of a new faith, who, when it was over, returned to their homes
bearing consecrated objects' – stones from the Bastille, engrav-
ings of the Rights of Man – which easily took the place of the
holy relics of peasant Catholicism (Leith, 1989, p. 172). Festivals themselves replaced other art forms in this period, for if
the Revolution left little by way of a permanent architectural
heritage, it invested heavily in artistic symbolism. Plays and
songs stressed the values of the secular and the glories of the
nation. And nearly a thousand painters and sculptors gave
artistic expression to the ethos of the times. In his heroic
portrayal of such revolutionary figures as Lepeletier and Marat,
for instance, Jacques-Louis David idealized the Revolution in
the manner of hagiography, turning their murders into 'visions
of sacrifice' (Roberts, 1989, p. 88).

   Political education was not all imposed from above. Indeed,
one of the characteristics of revolutions is that groups and
individuals within society themselves become politicized, often

going far beyond the norms admitted by the state. During the 1790s Frenchmen became more aware of their rights and of their powers as citizens. Elections played a part in this, since they accustomed a substantial section of society to the language of politics and invited them to take their share of political responsibility. Voting, however, was just one way in which people could participate in politics. They could read political opinion in any of the hundreds of newspapers which sprang up in Paris and the provinces during these years. For those unable to afford the relatively high subscriptions to the press, cafés began to buy papers for their customers and became meccas for political discussion. Even in the streets handbills and posters made passers-by aware of some of the burning issues of the day. All of a sudden, and most particularly in Paris, politics had become democratized through the printed word.

From the earliest months of the Revolution men of like views began to meet to discuss politics and to try to influence events. Soon groups were forming themselves into popular societies to press for political change or to pursue their own preferred causes. At national level there was a society to suit virtually every political taste – the Feuillants for constitutional monarchy and moderation, the Cordeliers for a more radical form of republicanism, the Club Massiac to defend the interests of the planters in the colonies, the Amis des Noirs to push for the freeing of slaves and the rights of blacks. As early as 1790 Breton deputies in Paris formed the Club Breton – the future Jacobins, soon to be the most powerful popular society of them all. Soon every provincial city of any importance could boast a number of rival societies, often loosely affiliated to those in the capital. Capitalizing on this proliferation of societies, the Paris Jacobins encouraged the formation of a network of clubs up and down France to whom they sent circulars and copies of resolutions and who formed the basis of a nation-wide Jacobin movement. It was to prove an invaluable resource, bringing Jacobin propaganda into even the smaller towns and villages of the south east and south west. In the twenty months before the Jacobin seizure of power in June 1793, Michael Kennedy calculates that clubs functioned in well over fifteen hundred communes, perhaps in as many as two thousand (Kennedy, 1988, p. 3). This network of clubs was to provide the Jacobins with a level of penetration unequalled by their rivals and gave them a national appeal which the Girondins were never able to match.

Clubs were closed societies composed of like-minded milit- ants. They had fixed memberships and collected subscriptions from their members. In contrast, the popular sections of France's larger cities were open meetings, open to all those resident in their catchment area. They had been created in 1790 as a simple measure of administrative convenience: Paris had been divided into 48 sections, for instance, Lyon and Marseille into 32, and Bordeaux into 28. They were not intended to enjoy any substantial political rights, but were seen as an essential part of the administrative structure needed to govern large urban areas. Soon, however, a number of the more radical Paris sections began to militate for political rights, most particularly the right to sit permanently and to choose their own agenda. When these concessions were finally granted, the sections became powerful pressure groups in their own right, discussing their own ideas and pursuing their own reforms even where these conflicted with the goals of the Assembly. By 1792 it was in the most radical of the sections that the Paris popular movement found its leaders and its organization. They fought for greater economic controls, for the punishment of specula- tors, for their own somewhat anarchic view of popular sover- eignty. They had their own newspapers and journalists, most notably Hébert's *Père Duchesne*; their own central mouthpiece in the Paris Commune; their own military force in the *armée révolutionnaire*. They prided themselves on their patriotism and the purity of their republican beliefs, and did not hesitate to challenge the government's centralist dogma. Both in Paris and in the larger provincial cities they were to show that they had their own leaders and political organization, their egalitarian beliefs and their ideas about social organization. They might form an alliance of convenience with the Montagnards; but

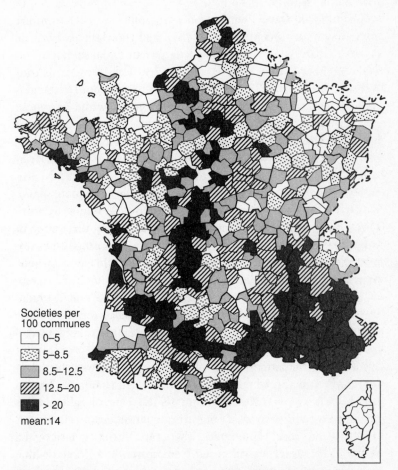

Figure 5 Numbers of political societies in Year II, by district
Source: Jean Boutier and Philippe Boutry, *Atlas de la Révolution Française,*
vol. 6 (Paris: Editions de l'Ecole des Hautes Etudes en Sciences Sociales,
1992).

their ideas remained their own. In Paris they continued to act as a pressure group for greater equality and economic terror, in defiance of the authorities. In Lyon, Marseille, and other provincial cities it was they who led the opposition of local people to what they saw as the insensitive tyranny of local Jacobin cadres. In no case were they a mere cipher of the national leadership.

They did, however, depend on a degree of support from the government, an acceptance that they had the right to meet, to discuss what issues they chose, to pay attendance money to their members. When these rights were withdrawn, and they were in the wake of Thermidor, the clubs and popular sections rapidly fell into decline. The Directory had few qualms about curbing the independence which they had enjoyed, and sheer boredom would seem to have killed off much of the radical press. 'What passed for public opinion', says Isser Woloch, 'was engrossed in exorcising sans-culottism, depantheonising Marat, and writing a new bourgeois constitution' (Woloch, 1970, p. 19). Unlike the men of 1793, the Thermidorians and Directorials had little interest in popular sovereignty or supposed rights to insurrection. They were concerned to establish the state on a stable footing, which involved root-and-branch reforms to the administration, the courts and the system of policing. In the more troublesome areas they made widespread use of the army, for internal policing as well as for the defence of France's frontiers. Napoleon, again seeking to end disorder, showed even less concern for participatory politics. Electoral participation was cut back. Opposition was ruthlessly repressed, and special courts were established to impose martial law in areas where lawlessness threatened. A new legal code was introduced which ironed out the contradictory clutter of statutes and local law codes that the Revolutionaries had bequeathed. Order was imposed from above on a France which was weary of political upheaval and which had lost faith in politicians. It was imposed in part by satisfying interests, in part by efficient administration; above all, it was imposed by force. But calm of a sort was created, so that a constitutional monarchist like Malouet could praise Napoleon for ending the squabbles and faction-fighting of the previous ten years. It was not, of course, the monarchy he so badly desired; but nor was it a return to autocracy. 'Today', wrote Malouet in 1800, 'the Consuls and their ministers curse factions, preaching political tolerance and justice and offering the promise of peace, which is the only true liberty' (Griffiths, 1988, p. 256).

4

Society

The Revolution of 1789 was primarily a political and constitutional revolution. But the revolutionaries realized that it would be impossible to bring about a revolution in the political order while leaving French society unscathed. They may have had no instant blueprint for social reform, yet the corporatist view of society which was so dominant during the *ancien régime* was incompatible with the ideas of political individualism which they saw as the centrepiece of the new order. What united many of the deputies to the Estates-General, and particularly the deputies to the Third Estate, was their shared opposition to the legal privilege on which political, economic and social relations were based. This does not mean that they saw themselves as social revolutionaries, far less that they would have denied the need for social inequalities. Indeed, the early months of the Revolution saw the publication of numerous books and pamphlets which argued that social inequalities were a natural characteristic of all societies and that they were necessary for social harmony. Rather they proposed to replace a society based on estates and birthright by one where merit and money would determine the status which the individual enjoyed. The equality of which they boasted was an equality of rights and opportunities. Men would have the same rights in law and receive the same treatment from the courts. They would be free to worship as they chose, with Protestants and Jews granted all the benefits of French citizenship; some Protestants, indeed – like the pastor Rabaut Saint-Etienne – would become prominent political figures during the Revolution. But distinctions would continue to be made between individuals, divisions that reflected work rate and ambition, skill and intelligence, for on such divisions did the stability of society itself depend. There was little that was socialist in the French Revolution. There could be no absolute equality, since men were unequal in so many fundamental ways.

Equality

'Men are born and remain free and equal in rights', proclaimed the first clause of the Declaration of the Rights of Man; but it said nothing about social or economic equality. Indeed the Declaration specifically defined the degree of equality which it deemed acceptable in a free society. Equality was not like liberty, an absolute political goal. It did not figure in the list of basic rights which were held to be self-evident in a free society: these were 'liberty, property, security and the resistance to oppression'. Property was sanctified as a 'sacred and inviolable right', however unequal its distribution amongst the community. And those without property were deemed not to have the necessary qualities for full citizenship. This was, as Louis Bergeron has recently pointed out, a natural enough assumption in the enlightened circles of the later eighteenth century. D'Holbach had commented that a man who owns nothing in the state will be tied by no links with society (Lucas, 1991, p. 128). Indeed, one of the legacies of the Enlightenment was the replacement of the idea of privilege with that of property as the cement which guaranteed the solidity of social institutions. Society was still to be stratified, but stratified according to wealth, property ownership, economic utility. Once again this principle was enshrined in the Rights of Man, which stated clearly that 'social distinctions should be founded only on communal utility' (Stewart, 1951, pp. 113–15). There was little dissent, even amongst Patriots and Republicans. The revolutionaries might disagree bitterly as to the nature of these distinctions and the true meaning of equality, but there were few among them who saw economic equality as a realistic – or even as a desirable – social goal. Where many of them did agree was in their commitment to some idea of community. The individual must be freed from the constraints of *ancien régime* privilege; but – in Jacobin eyes at least – an equal society was one where the excesses of individualism would be controlled by a prevailing sense of communal interest.

It may be questioned, indeed, whether any politician during the 1790s conceived of an equal society in an economic sense. The Constituents were too busy defining categories of citizenship and restricting electoral participation; they were not egalitarians. Among republicans, too, few were really interested in equality other than in its legal manifestations. As Roederer recognized in his *Esprit de la Révolution*, between an equality of rights and real equality there was a huge and often unbridgeable gulf (Furet and Ozouf, 1988, p. 696). Both Girondins and Jacobins declared their support for a free-market economy, as the freedom to move goods without constraint was regarded as a fundamental aspect of revolutionary liberty. Economic liberalism, indeed, was posited as an essential form of individual freedom, the antithesis of the corporate privileges and royal monopolies that had characterized the eighteenth century. This had clear implications for society, too. In a free society, the duty of the state was to regulate rather than to intrude. The law was there to guarantee the individual rights and to limit the centralizing instincts of authority. Gradually, of course, the state began to reassert itself. The needs of war contributed powerfully to this change, as recruitment, billeting, and requisition all placed increased obligations on the individual. Under the Jacobin Republic these demands became more exigent. The dutes of citizenship were increasingly emphasized, often to the detriment of rights and liberties. Good citizens had to fulfil their obligations to the state; they had to be concerned for the public interest and the public good. Citizenship came increasingly to be defined in terms of virtue.

This emphasis on individual rights was not shared by all. Some had every interest in the maintenance of a degree of protection and regulation, not least those who saw themselves reduced to penury by unrestrained competition. Among the peasantry, for instance, were many small proprietors who loathed the rural bourgeoisie, especially those whose wealth posed a threat to their own well-being; there were many among them who rushed to welcome Jacobin schemes for *partage* and the equal division of the commons. Others again realized that their continued viability depended on the maintenance of common lands on which to graze their animals and clung to their traditional communal ways. Such people were not imbued with a capitalist ethic; they did not understand fully fledged individualism and were poorly equipped to cope with a free market in grain and farm produce. Indeed, if the revolutionaries were perceived as advocates of capitalism they risked being rejected in large areas of the countryside. Hence the failure of many urban clubs to recruit in rural areas. Where Jacobin clubs were formed in the countryside it was often by giving them over to the demands of the peasantry. A good instance is the local club at Arpajon in the Cantal, the *Société des hommes de la nature*, created in 1791 by Jean-Baptiste Milhaud. The society flourished and became a hub of rural radicalism, but it was no ordinary Jacobin club. Milhaud built on the grievances of the peasants in an area long prone to rural *jacqueries*, to he point where the club ceased to speak the language of the towns and became a vehicle for peasant demands concerning taxation and feudal dues (Jones, 1988, p. 214).

The Parisian *sans-culottes* were another group who had little reason to support the free market, since many of them feared the commercial challenge of large-scale enterprise. But were they committed egalitarians? This depends to some extent on the definition we adopt. Many of them were opposed to excessive wealth, just as they disliked ostentation. In

Vingternier's famous definition, a *sans-culotte* was someone 'who always goes on foot, who does not have any millions stashed away, no castles, no valets to wait upon him, and who lives quite simply with his wife and children, if he has any, on the fourth or the fifth floor' (Markov and Soboul, 1957, p. 2). Some sections specified that one man should not own more than one workshop. To that degree they were egalitarian, opposed to excessive wealth, insisting that those who worked hard were entitled to an adequate livelihood. But in no sense were they opposed to private property, for on private property their own status depended. Some of them were men of substantial property themselves, like Santerre the brewer, who was a considerable employer of labour. Others were small craftsmen and shopkeepers whose livelihood depended on their mastery of their trade; they too valued their economic independence and had no interest in a blanket economic equality imposed from the centre. At most what they wanted was protection from the worst abuses of free enterprise – price controls on bread and other essentials in times of shortage; checks on peasant producers who wanted to sell their crops elsewhere; laws forbidding the export of grain stocks; or punitive taxes on the rich, on hoarders and speculators, on those whom they regarded as enjoying an undeservedly large share of the national cake. Theirs was almost a moral stance, a revulsion that the few should have such incommensurate economic power, a belief that income and disposable wealth should be in some way related to the everyday needs of an ordinary family. But they were not in any sense socialists, and their platform was at no time that of enforced equality (Cobb, 1969, pp. 122–41). To expect otherwise is to misrepresent the revolutionary mind: enforced equality meant greater controls, and the Revolution was essentially devoted to removing controls, which were too easily identified with royal tyranny. Legislation might be introduced to avert the worst social injustices, but where liberty and equality were in conflict it was liberty which would be favoured.

There were, of course, exceptions to this rule. Robespierre

was one political leader who recognized that there were circumstances which made it necessary to curtail freedom in the interests of more equitable distribution, as his support for the General Maximum and the Ventôse Decrees demonstrates. But this can also be seen as a political manoeuvre to win the support of the Paris sections at a time when republican opinion, both in the Convention and in the country, was increasingly divided. Economic egalitarianism was for most of the Revolution equated with extremism, with a view of politics that had little to do with the work of government. It implied a denial of the sacred rights of property which were accepted by all mainstream politicians. It was left to sectional extremists like Jacques Roux to talk of declaring open war on the rich; or to radical journalists like Marat and Hébert. But even they emphasized the political over the economic, as did the supporters of the rights of slaves or the early feminists of the women's clubs. One of the few popular leaders to preach anything approaching economic equality was Gracchus Babeuf, who roundly denounced meritocracy and advocated a more strictly egalitarian division of wealth in accordance with individual need. Babeuf was consistent in his egalitarian beliefs. As a democratic agitator in Picardy he had championed greater peasant equality by denying individual ownership of farming land; and he urged that other property be redistributed more equitably to satisfy the needs of the population at large. After Thermidor, in the words of R. B. Rose, he strove, 'as a journalist and pamphleteer, to rally the scattered and demoralised democratic forces against both the remnants of the revolutionary government and the steady political counteroffensive of the bourgeois conservatives' (Rose 1978, p. 345). And he demanded that the Jacobin constitution of 1793 should finally be enacted. His writings would leave a deep mark on early nineteenth-century socialists, but at the time his was an isolated voice in the wilderness. His attempted rising in 1796, rapidly followed by his trial and execution, signalled the end of any serious egalitarian movement during the Directory.

Reform of society and abolition of privilege

This does not mean, however, that the Revolution was uninterested in economic and social reform. On the contrary, some of the most pungent criticisms levelled against the *ancien régime*, both in the *cahiers de doléances* and in the speeches of revolutionary politicians, were criticisms of the existing social order. For *ancien régime* society was seen as being the product of legal privilege, a society based upon legal estates and cemented by a strict corporatist structure. And though the privileged orders were not totally exclusive, like castes, entry to them had been jealously guarded: a rich commoner might hope to purchase nobility, for example – and merchants were increasingly tempted to do so in the course of the eighteenth century – but membership of the Second Estate remained a royal prerogative, to be granted sparingly either for cash or for service to the monarchy. At all levels of society rights and status were determined by privilege, usually by privilege conferred by the King. The aristocracy and clergy enjoyed exemptions from taxation through privilege; tax farmers made huge profits as a result of a privileged role which they had purchased from the monarchy; charters granted to particular trading companies guaranteed a monopoly of certain markets; gilds and *corporations* jealously maintained their privileged position over the world of work. Gild members might defend their privilege as a necessary defence of standards and craft skills; but those who remained on the outside, who had not served their apprenticeship or been admitted to the charmed circle of the corporation, saw the system as a restrictive practice which curtailed freedom of trade and which inflated the profits of the few.

Much of the early work of the Revolution consisted in the abolition of privilege and the demolition of the corporatist structure of *ancien régime* society. In particular, the Revolution turned its attention to the privileges enjoyed by the nobility and to the grievances of the peasantry over feudal dues and indemnities. There was widespread agreement that privileges derived from a man's membership of the Second Estate had no moral or political justification, and as early as 7 November a decree was passed abolishing social orders in France. Now everyone would be a citizen and equally liable to fulfil fiscal demands. Taxes would no longer be on the person but on land, property, and trading profits. There was strong demand, too, that feudal dues be abolished in keeping with the new spirit of equality before the law. The move for abolition began in dramatic form during the night of 4 August 1789, when noble after noble rose to his feet in the National Assembly to renounce his privileges. This scene would be powerfully symbolic during the years that followed: it is enshrined in some of the most famous etchings and caricatures of the entire Revolution. But the degree to which real change was attained should not be exaggerated. The aristocrats were acting out of fear as much as from magnanimity, with wild and often exaggerated reports reaching Paris of the ravages of peasant destruction. And when their fear passed, many of the rights which had been so lightly jettisoned were reimposed. The real process of abolition would be a much slower and more ponderous effort of legislation, spread over a number of years. More seriously for the peasants, the law which finally abolished seigneurial dues made a clear distinction between those dues which were to be simply abolished and those which – because they were regarded as property – had to be redeemed, often by payments that far exceeded the capabilities of the rural population. And rents, of course, still had to be honoured, even if the immediate reaction of many tenants had been to suspend all forms of payment to their landlords (Jones, 1988, pp. 86–123).

It was not just the privileges of the aristocracy that were under attack; it was the entire notion of privilege which was anathema to a nation of free men, regardless of the benefits it might confer. The free movement of persons and goods was therefore assured, without tolls or tariffs or other forms of constraint. Trading company privileges were abolished, allowing all to trade freely on an equal footing. Prices were to be fixed by the market without government intervention, since intervention seemed redolent of the role played by the

Intendant during the *ancien régime*. Municipal and provincial privileges were also abolished, despite the reservations voiced by local *notables*. Bordeaux could no longer refuse to accept beer at the city gates; the Roussillon could not evoke ancient exemptions from militia service. The Revolutionaries believed in the free market, that all must be free to trade on equal terms, without exercising special privileges or restrictive practices. Much of their economic and social legislation was designed to abolish such practices and to ensure the free movement of goods – until, of course, the declaration of war made new controls necessary and established new priorities for the state. But these controls were seldom voluntary. They were seen as short-term measures made necessary by the crisis – by the demand for supplies, the need for requisitions, or the near-starvation of the cities. They were never part of revolutionary ideology.

What applied to traders and civic dignitaries also applied to the workforce. The corporate society of the eighteenth century must give way to individualism. Gilds were therefore abolished as prejudicial to free trade, and master craftsmen were forced to compete with those from outside the walls, the immigrant tradesmen of the Parisian *faubourgs*. Since work, like virtually every aspect of eighteenth-century life, was organized on a corporate basis – the gilds represented every group from carpenters to barristers – this measure promised to effect a revolutionary change in working practices. Nor were its effects limited to the workshop masters who ran the gilds; it also prejudiced the rights of the workforce. Journeymen and apprentices were deprived of their traditional associations, the *compagnonnages* which had organized their *tour de France* and to which they had turned for succour when labour disputes erupted. It is arguable, indeed, that it was the ordinary craftsman who was most seriously harmed by the uncompromising individualism of the period, since, with the Loi Le Chapelier of June 1791, he was denied any collective representation that might help defend his interests. Le Chapelier made no secret of his intentions. When he introduced his measure in the

Assembly he denounced meetings of workers of a single trade who were using their collective strength to increase wage rates or to improve working conditions: they were, he said, attempting to recreate illegal organizations under a new name, holding masters to ransom and threatening the use of violence. Groups of artisans were passing resolutions, appointing presidents and secretaries, keeping regular minutes. His decree made all such meetings illegal, as being contrary to the spirit of the Revolution. And workers, in line with the free-market philosophy of the regime, were left without any form of protection in future labour disputes.

What to its proponents was the benefit of a free market in skills and labour could appear to those deprived of their gilds as little better than economic anarchy. A good example is provided by the Paris book trades, which were duly deregulated in accordance with revolutionary policy. Printers and publishers, freed from the controls of the Paris Book Guild, at first revelled in the freedoms afforded them. The years 1790 and 1791 were ones of high demand for pamphlets and tracts, and the removal of censorship encouraged a flurry of activity. But if small print shops sprang into existence, often hopelessly under-capitalized, the book trade floundered, and by the Year II the entire printing industry was threatened by a crushing economic recession (Hesse, 1991, p. 135). It is instructive that by the end of the Revolution those publishers who had survived often asked the government for the restoration of some controlling mechanism to save them from bankruptcy. Economic individualism, it seemed, was not the panacea the revolutionaries had supposed. Besides, if the corporate structures disappeared after 1791, the social problems which had led gildsmen to such widespread litigation in the eighteenth century did not. Conflicts within the trades, disputes over debts, the maintenance of supplies, and a host of other problems continued to exercise the workshop masters long after 1791 (Sonenscher, 1989, p. 294). There was little reason for goldsmiths or cabinet-makers to denounce their gilds or to welcome the new revolutionary law. Nor was affection for the gilds restricted to tradespeople; the professions, too, resisted the changes which the Revolution forced upon them. In Paris the former *avocats au parlement* made no secret of their preference for the corporate idiom to which they were accustomed (Fitzsimmons, 1987, pp. 88–9). In Toulouse the majority of the barristers saw their salvation in withdrawal from the new institutional order (Berlanstein, 1975, p. 182).

Clerical privilege, too, was ripe for assault. The clergy, like the aristocracy, enjoyed significant tax privileges, in particular the right of self-taxation; they were the recipients of the much-hated tithe; and the Church was a huge landowner in its own right. Overall it may have owned between 6 and 10 per cent of the land area of France, though this figure rose to over 30 per cent in Picardy and the Cambrésis (McManners, 1969, p. 6). The upper clergy were often as involved in court politics as they were in the saving of souls: many of the bishops were little interested by administration, while abbeys and monasteries were widely attacked for their wealth and their irrelevance to social needs. As an institution, the Church had allowed itself to become identified with the monarchy, to the extent that some of the more anti-clerical of the *philosophes* saw their fate as being inextricably linked. Even in those areas of social life where the Church played an important role – such as poor relief and education – demographic pressures and the unevenness of resourcing led to criticism. Besides, Catholic traditions lay at the very heart of eighteenth-century French culture, and they were traditions which emphasized inequality and order, obedience and hierarchy. Just as the Church's political position proved incompatible with the Revolution's claims to national sovereignty, so in the social sphere Church and state proved uneasy bedfellows. When in 1791 a substantial part of the clergy refused to take the oath of loyalty to the new regime under the Civil Constitution of the Clergy, preferring emigration and exile, the remaining bonds between Church and state were seriously damaged (Tackett, 1986). In spite of any lingering deism which Robespierre may have felt – and the Cult of the Supreme Being suggests strongly that he was not without

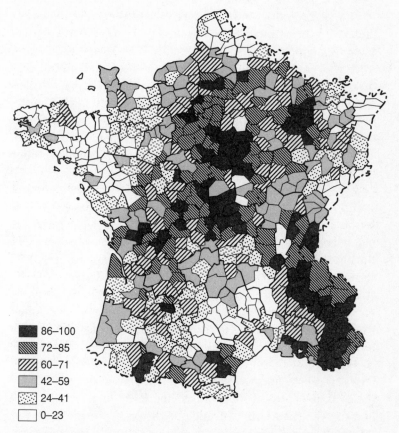

■	86–100
▨	72–85
▨	60–71
▨	42–59
▧	24–41
□	0–23

Figure 6 Percentages of clergy who accepted the Civil Constitution
(spring–summer 1791), by district
Source: T. Tackett, *Religion, Revolution and Regional Culture in Eighteenth-
century France: The Ecclesiastical Oath of 1791* (Princeton University
Press, 1986).

faith – the First Republic would be based on largely secular foundations.

Undermining the privileged order of the *ancien régime* was a considerable legislative task, and one that the revolutionaries set about with enthusiasm. Much of the permissive legislation of the years from 1789 to 1791 was effectively devoted to freeing Frenchmen from existing bonds of deference and social obligation. But just how should the old, privileged and stratified society of the *ancien régime* be replaced? What should be the underlying principles of the new social order? The revolutionaries desperately needed to establish new social parameters, since they were no more anarchists in the social sphere than they were in politics. Peasants as well as townspeople, villagers as well as citizens, all had to be educated in the new values of revolutionary citizenship, all had to transfer to the new order their traditional respect for the king, the seigneur, and the *curé*. The individual gained civil – and with it social – status through his role as a citizen.

What they sought to create was a society in which status would be closely identified with service, with duties performed in the cause of the Revolution. And service was not restricted to a narrow elite, as had been the case under the Bourbons: the Revolution created a more open society, where careers were accessible to talent and social mobility was dramatically increased. These were values, of course, which greatly favoured the bourgeoisie, those men of commerce and the professions who attached themselves to the revolutionary cause. That is not to dismiss the entire Revolution as a bourgeois movement. But it is to suggest that often there was no incompatibility between liberal idealism and the self-interest of those who now found themselves in power. One does not have to subscribe to a Marxist view of history to conclude that many of the economic reforms of the 1790s, from the abolition of tolls and privileges to the banning of gilds and journeymen's associations, were, in Colin Jones's formulation, 'classically capitalistic in their character' (Lucas, 1991, p. 114). Nor is it necessary to exaggerate the tension that existed between the commercial and professional elites. In the later eighteenth century there is evidence of growing interaction between them, of shared interests and a growing economic interdependence. In some towns they even made common cause on political matters. William Scott's study of the merchants of Marseille shows how in the elections to the National Assembly they could claim to represent all 'industry', including the small independent artisan, and could talk of trade as a 'rampart against despotism', a source of social equality and a bastion against privilege (Forrest and Jones, 1991, p. 88). The interest of lawyers and the liberal professions in the cause of reform is easier to demonstrate. Some, it is true, had wealth and status bound up in the privileged structures of the *ancien régime*, in their service to the Crown or to the various courts of the *parlements*. But they were a minority. Most shared the enthusiasm of the National Assembly for the cause of careers open to talent, a cause which presented them with a myriad of new opportunities. Their interests could easily be submerged in the wider ideological cause that was the Revolution.

The Revolution and the aristocracy

There would of course be losers as well as winners in the Revolution's social programme, the aristocracy, in particular, finding little to attract them to the new social norms. Some might argue that they were given little encouragement to do so: from the very outset they were identified with *ancien régime* privilege and regarded as potential enemies of reform. Patrice Higonnet makes this point well, showing how consistently the revolutionaries maintained their attack on noble values and noble rights. For if the Revolution prided itself on its open society, it did not pretend to tolerance. Freedom and meritocracy were linked to political morality, and nobles were offered little quarter. The attack on their status began early. On the night of 4 August their privileges were abolished; and a year later any vestige of nobility disappeared in law. Henceforth nobles were just private citizens, without either special rights or social status. Their nobility counted for nothing. And their sufferings did not end there. Many of them emigrated; many more withdrew from every aspect of public life. Following the flight of the King and the treachery of many noble army officers, their lot worsened further, as the revolutionaries came to see former nobles – '*ci-devants*' – as potential counter-revolutionaries. During the Jacobin Republic aristocracy itself came to be regarded as a crime, as evidence that a man was unreliable and should be treated as a suspect. In the months of the Terror society came to reflect more narrowly the ideology of those in power, a man's status being dependent on his political loyalty and on his civic worth – the payment of taxes, service with the National Guard, attendance at sections and political involvement through political clubs. These were not tests which the aristocracy were well placed to pass, and many of them found themselves imprisoned or dragged before revolutionary tribunals. But even then their ordeal was not over. Long after the fall of the Jacobins, in November 1797, the Directory flaunted its anti-noble credentials by depriving all nobles – 'including babes in arms' – of French citizenship (Higonnet, 1981, p. 1). Henceforth nobility was incompatible with membership of the national community; the process of exclusion which had begun in 1789 had been completed.

The lot of the aristocracy is symptomatic in another way, too. Like political reform, social reform during the revolutionary years was something to be achieved by legislative coercion. Whole batteries of laws were passed creating the infrastructure of a liberal economic and social order and denying the aristocracy and clergy their time-honoured position in society. At local level, as with the new political order, social change was to be assured by education and propaganda. Republican schoolmasters were to replace priests in the classroom and were to preach a secular republican catechism. In hospitals, too, the role of religion came under strict surveillance, with almoners suspended from their duties and nursing sisters carefully supervised lest they try to indoctrinate the sick and dying. Anything openly reminiscent of the old order was scorned. Symbols of monarchy and aristocracy – such as inscriptions and coats of arms – were chipped off public buildings by armies of stonemasons. Public demonstrations of fraternity were encouraged and carefully staged. Even the language of everyday discourse was subtly changed in a bid to remove any remaining symptoms of deference or oligarchy. By 1794 mayors were supposed to report to their superiors every ten days outlining the state of public opinion in their communes and drawing attention to any likely threat to the social order. And the judgements of revolutionary tribunals against hoarders and aristocrats were intended to have a normative social value as well as to press home a clear political message. Judgements were well publicized, with printed wall posters bringing political cases to the notice of the community at large. Executions were intended to be very public events, themselves an exercise in public exorcism. The purpose of all these measures was clear: to create a new man, uncontaminated by the corruption of the eighteenth-century world. By a myriad of measures, some crude and brutal, others subtly psychological, the old social structure was to be undermined and the values of France's new civic order impressed on the people.

Though it would be foolish to exaggerate the impact of this social revolution – the history of the nineteenth century suggests greater continuity than we might expect – its short-term impact is not in doubt. A society based on birth was largely replaced by a society based on function: men were to be judged by what they did rather than by who they were. The old elites of the Church and the aristocracy either went into emigration or accepted that their once-powerful functions had been marginalized. In contrast, the urban bourgeois saw opportunity on every side – in trade, in the law, and in politics. They were likely to play a major role in local politics, both at communal and at district level; they staffed the national guard, served on revolutionary committees and tribunals, and held office in local Jacobin clubs. Economically they might hope to benefit from the liberalization of the economy, and they could, if they so chose, hope to buy up land in the surrounding countryside.

Money and a certain shrewdness were their passports to material success, and many of them took advantage of the sales of national lands to acquire valuable properties at knock-down prices. If the nobles were the clearest losers from the Revolution, the bourgeois – and especially, perhaps, those from the smaller towns and market centres – were the clearest winners. Their literacy gave them access to news and to office, while their advanced ideas found support in Paris. By the Year II they often exercised considerable power in their localities, imposing anti-clerical policies and forcing others to toe their line. They were the *cadres* of the Revolution, the small-town and village *notables*.

The Revolution and the poor

But what of the poorer groups in eighteenth-century society, the peasants and labourers in the countryside, the journeymen and workers in the cities? Did the social policy of the Revolution do much to benefit them or to provide them with greater opportunity? The peasants had had high expectations after the preparation of the *cahiers*, but were these expectations realistic, and was the Revolution interested in fulfilling them? In some respects it is clear that it was – the abolition of tithes and of some at least of the feudal dues, the removal of onerous tolls and *octrois*, and the ending of the iniquities of the system of tax farming all provided clear benefits for society at large. But once again, these were legal changes – the sort of changes that a legislative regime is best equipped to make – rather than economic ones. In fact the rural economy stagnated for much of the decade, with notably poor harvests in the early 1790s, and recurrent crises affecting cereals, viticulture, and animal husbandry. Indeed, the enduring memory of the 1790s was one of hardship and poverty. Nor was this compensated for by the Revolution's much-vaunted land policy. The amount of land made available to the poorer peasantry from the sale of *biens nationaux* was often quite minimal, whereas the richer *labou-*

reurs and urban bourgeois could invest in large plots or round up their existing holdings. For the government's primary aim in ordering the sales was not redistribution but fund raising for the war effort; only during the Jacobin months was some effort made to use national lands for social purposes, and the pattern of peasant gains varied greatly from one region to another. In other respects the Revolution's property laws could even seem destructive of the peasant patrimony. Its insistence on equal inheritance by all children, though patently fair and giving unparalleled rights to girls and to illegitimate children, was seen as a curse by smallholders: they knew that many of their plots were not capable of subdivision and feared that the result would be destitution. As for the Jacobin policy of *partage* – the division of common lands among the individual plotholders – it was greeted very differently in different sorts of farming community. Popular in the granary belt of the north, it had little relevance in many of the *pays de petite culture* of the Massif or the south west, where the maintenance of common lands was vital to continued economic viability (Jones, 1988, pp. 144–6).

Nor did revolutionary policies always work to the benefit of the urban artisan or unskilled labourer. It is true that he would be given political and civil rights and that he might participate in the work of his section. But economically the interests of workers were barely compatible with the free market which the Revolution tried to create. They needed protection against slump and unemployment, and protection for their trade against unscrupulous employers. They wanted cheap bread, a controlled market in staples in which they would not be exploited by hoarders and speculators. They demanded that the government impose controls on suppliers, that they prevent the rich from hoarding grain, peasants from holding back supplies, millers from perpetrating frauds. They needed guaranteed supplies of raw materials to exercise their trade, and raw materials at an affordable price. In short, they wanted the government to act as a regulator of the market, to impose controls and conditions on commerce, and to punish those who exploited their economic power: they were constantly afraid of a recurrence of the time-honoured *pacte de famine* (Kaplan, 1982, pp. 1–4). For many among them the position was only made worse by the abolition of their trade organizations, which they felt left them naked and unprotected. These economic differences help explain the gulf which opened up between the politics of revolutionary governments – all the governments of the period, even that of the Jacobins – and the leaders of the radical sections of Paris. Only briefly, during 1793 and 1794, did the sections succeed in imposing a policy of economic controls as the price of their alliance. When that alliance broke down and the Jacobins were overthrown, the *sans-culottes* were left impotent and the people they represented were again exposed to the rigours of the market. By the winter of 1795 the extent of these rigours were clear to all. The terrible conditions of that winter, during which the Seine was frozen over for weeks on end, condemned many to cold, misery and near starvation. Firewood stocks were exhausted, and some sixty thousand Parisians depended for their survival on hand-outs of subsidized bread. *Nonante-cinq* haunted Parisian imaginations. For the poor it was a pungent symbol of the revolutionary free market.

Throughout the *ancien régime* the great fear of poor families, both in the towns and in the countryside, had been the fear of poverty – of falling below the breadline, generally through no fault of their own, as a result of illness or the death of a breadwinner, loss of employment, or simply a bad harvest. They feared that their economy of makeshifts would fail, that they would face the misery of homelessness and dependence on institutional charity. To them the Revolution, with its humanitarian emphasis on liberty and human dignity, seemed to offer new hope; and the Comité de Mendicité of the Constituent Assembly encouraged that hope by carrying out extensive research into the extent of poverty and suggesting ambitious legislative solutions. The revolutionaries saw poverty as a problem for the nation, its relief as a 'sacred debt' which governments could not shirk (Hufton, 1974, pp. 22–4). For the revolutionary leaders believed poverty to be incompatible with liberty, and argued that the continued existence of human misery was a slur upon the good name of the Revolution itself. Their solutions, though heavily influenced by the experiments of the *ancien régime*, showed great imagination. They drew a clear distinction between the deserving and undeserving poor and had little time for the workshy, but for the majority of the country's poor they proposed *bienfaisance* as a matter of right. Hospitals and hospices should look after the old and sick, workshops were opened to provide jobs for the unemployed, and greater emphasis was placed on assistance at home, on money payments that would allow the deserving poor to stay in their own communities. It was a policy aimed at overcoming short-term economic crises, the cyclical crises which tradition-ally afflicted large numbers of peasant families. It was also a policy which implied a degree of trust: the poor did not have to be supervised or institutionalized – with all the loss of freedom and petty humiliation which that implied – in order to receive aid. Instead, they were seen as citizens to whom the state had urgent responsibilities (Forrest, 1981, pp. 13–33).

The failure of the Revolution's social policy

If this ambitious policy failed it was not because of any lack of political will. Rather, the failure of social policy must be ascribed to the Revolution's inability to control the economy. From the very outset the regime faced mounting economic difficulties. It started in crisis, the crisis which in 1787 and 1788 had helped bring down the *ancien régime*. It inherited the debts of royal governments, and the National Assembly made it known that it would honour these debts, even though the cost would be a millstone round the neck of the revolutionary authorities. Poor harvests during the immediately preceding years not only led to popular disturbances; they also meant that peasants consumed the seedcorn which should have been put aside for the future and that the early Revolution was condemned to mediocre food yields. The Revolution itself added further difficulties. The abolition of some feudal dues and the promised abolition of others led to confusion as well as rejoicing, with the consequence that tax revenues fell sharply. Nor could these lost revenues be easily replaced through borrowing, since creditors had little reason to have confidence in a country in turmoil. The first years of the Revolution saw the French tax base evaporate as many of the richest nobles left for emigration, laden with gold, silver and precious objects. If many of the peasants withheld their taxes, skilled artisans such as the silk-weavers of Lyon followed their customers to Switzerland or Germany. Worse was to follow with the declaration of war. Resources were increasingly diverted into war industries and to supplying the nation's armies, while commerce and agriculture suffered from both a loss of manpower and a loss of markets. The extension of the land war to include Britain in the spring of 1793 dealt a particularly savage blow to France's Atlantic trade; ports like Nantes, Bordeaux and La Rochelle saw their economies enter a period of savage decline as British warships and privateers cut them off from the Americas and from the West Indian sugar islands.

As a result, a succession of French governments was forced to look to non-traditional means of raising revenue. These governments turned to their own people for voluntary donations; they placed levies on the rich; they seized the property of those who had emigrated. But these could only be stop-gap measures. More crucial was the decision to issue a new paper currency, the *assignat*, whose value would be sustained not by holdings of gold and silver but by sales of national lands, against which the paper could, at least theoretically, be exchanged. Acceptance of the *assignat* soon came to be seen as a test of patriotism and revolutionary virtue. All revolutionary governments from the Constituent Assembly to the Directory found themselves forced to make paper the basis of their economic management; without it they would have been unable to finance their ambitious public programmes.

But the policy was fraught with dangers. It soon became

evident that the Revolution did not really understand the full implications of a paper currency, and many politicians, among them Necker, expressed their fears publicly. How many *assignats* should be issued? Could they circulate alongside the existing specie? In what units should they be issued? And how could the government persuade people to accept them? These were major problems in a country where a large part of the population had little experience of using money in any form; agriculture in many areas was largely of a subsistence kind, and there barter still flourished. Yet Paris believed it could persuade peasants who seldom used coin that they should have confidence in printed paper bills. The first reactions were hardly promising. Employers complained that the paper money had been distributed in far too large units, so that they could not pay daily wages; some even tried tearing up the *assignats* to provide the sums they required. Abroad it proved impossible to force merchants to accept them, and even at home many insisted on being paid in bullion. Soon the value of the paper was eroded by inflation, and prices came to be quoted at two different levels, one for coin, the other for paper. Confidence quickly drained away. Yet government officials and contractors were often forced to use paper; and payments to hospitals, state pensions and wages to those working in the public sector were made only in *assignats*. As their value fell, so the poor became poorer, until under the Directory many hospitals complained that they were reduced to total penury. They had neither food nor drink, bandages nor medical supplies; there were no sheets or bedding, and buildings were left to decay; nurses and doctors went unpaid for months, and when money finally arrived it had lost most of its value. As a result of the government's economic failures the social policy of the Revolution lay in tatters.

Inflation was the principal problem, created in part by the over-issue of *assignats* to finance government spending, but even more by a deep-seated lack of confidence which made people reluctant to accept paper or to hang on to it once they had it. This had been evident to some deputies as early as 1790 when the issue was debated in the Assembly. For if the radicals

favoured the use of *assignats* as a means of financing revolutionary legislation, the more financially conservative counselled
caution. Dupont de Nemours was one who incurred the wrath
of radicals by suggesting that only the rich would benefit from
the issue, since they would be able to buy up national lands at
bargain prices, paying for them in devalued currency, while the
people faced steeply rising bread prices (Aftalion, 1990, p. 81).
But few listened; already the issue had come to be a political
shibboleth, and the Constituent was committed to paper. Yet
Dupont's counsels had been wise. The flooding of the land
market with *biens nationaux* did depress land prices. And the
real value of the currency did spiral downwards. If it was
quoted at parity (100) in June 1790, its value was cut to only
22 per cent of face value by the summer of 1793. The Jacobin
government and the institution of Terror helped staunch the
flow, so that by Thermidor the *assignat* had risen again, to a
peak of 48 per cent. But after Robespierre's fall, hyperinflation
set in. By the summer of 1795 the value of the *assignat* fell
below 3 per cent, and within months it became effectively
valueless. The Directory, desperate for income, abandoned the
assignat and sought to redeem a large part of its debt by the
issue of a further experiment in paper currency, the *mandat
territorial*. Valued at thirty times the *assignat*, this was supposed
to have an equivalent value in gold. But the public remained
sceptical and the *mandat* rapidly lost all credibility.

The Revolution and women

The lack of public funds may have stopped public-works
programmes and curbed government spending on the poor and
the sick. But not all social legislation required public investment, especially since some of the most radical revolutionary
ideas concerned social rights and public attitudes. The approach adopted towards women is especially instructive. In civil
matters the revolutionaries recognized that women ought to
enjoy greater rights than in the past, especially in the private

domain. Why should wives obey husbands without question or bear injury without complaint? Why should property pass to sons rather than to daughters and to the eldest son rather than to the others? Why should the greatest educational opportunities be reserved for boys? Why – other than for reasons of Catholic tradition – should aggrieved partners not resolve their marital problems through divorce? During the revolutionary period man and wife came to enjoy a new degree of equality before the law. Wives could buy, sell and inherit property. All children were given equal rights of inheritance. State schooling was provided for girls as well as boys. And the institution of divorce led to the liberation of many women from unhappy and tyrannical marriages (Phillips, 1981, pp. 196–203). The revolutionary political order might still be overwhelmingly a male domain – indeed, it is arguable that Revolutionary anti-clericalism and the forced closure of churches actually discriminated against women and their interests – but the revolutionary social order was more even-handed in its treatment of the sexes (Hunt, 1984, p. 109).

That is not to suggest that women were treated as the equals of men, for there were spheres of activity from which they continued to be systematically excluded. At no time during the Revolution did women obtain full rights of citizenship, and there was little call for them to be granted the vote. The women's clubs which did exist were pale shadows of their male counterparts, struggling with tiny attendance figures to attract some degree of attention for their cause. And they were largely ignored by the revolutionaries, who sought to exclude them from political decision making. In this respect the Jacobins were even less tolerant than their predecessors, and in the autumn of 1793 the process of removing women from the public sphere was virtually complete. They were explicitly excluded from citizenship; their political organizations were banned; they were even forbidden to appear before the Convention to state their case. The role of women in public life was to be a symbolic one only. For, as Sarah Melzer and Leslie Rabine have recently observed, 'at the same time that women were expelled from the public sphere, Woman as an allegorical figure came more and more pervasively to stand for Liberty, Equality, republican virtues, and the republic itself in men's representations of the new political order' (Melzer and Rabine, 1992, p. 5). The male body of the King was replaced by the female symbol of the Goddess of Liberty in revolutionary iconography.

In Paris sectional radicals were little inclined to admit their wives and daughters to political activism. Their popular image of the patriotic woman was firmly defined within the domestic sphere. She was honest and faithful, a good cook and the mother of a family; her place was at home, educating the children in republican principles, not in the bars or sectional meeting halls frequented by her husband. Hébert, in his *Père Duchesne*, provides a splendidly stereotyped vision of *sans-culotte* family life which leaves little doubt that the woman's principal role was that of furnishing support. For the *sans-culotte* finds comfort and solace in his family after a hard day in the workshop. 'In the evening, when he returns to his garret, his wife leaps on his shoulder, his little brats run to kiss him, his dog jumps up to lick his face. He tells them the news he has learned at his section. . . . Then he eats his supper with a hearty appetite and after his meal he regales his family with excerpts from the Père Duchesne' (Hardman, 1973, p. 218). Women were not expected to play an active role in revolution, and when they did the authorities took fright. When in May 1793 a group of militant women founded their own popular society, the *Club des Citoyennes Républicaines*, with the stated aim of working to prevent hoarding and speculation in food, the Committee of Public Safety was anxious. It raised the dual spectre of working women taking to the streets of Paris and of a possible alliance between the women of the markets and the more extreme Enragés, like Jacques Roux, whose agenda they shared (Hufton, 1992, p. 25).

But however much republican politicians might have preferred to exclude women from the political sphere, women did play a significant part in the Revolution, especially in popular *journées* and in market disturbances. They were not mere passive onlookers; nor were they the court intriguers of the *ancien régime*. In part, of course, their role was one that was traditional to women. They protested at high bread prices and demanded the opening of public workshops. They were responsible for manning revolutionary hospitals. They kept production going while their husbands went off to fight on the frontiers. But their role did not stop there. In the October Days of 1789, it was the women of Paris – if Mercier is to be believed, twenty thousand of them – who marched to Versailles to bring the King and his family back to Paris. Their intervention was a decisive one which served to advance the Revolution and to reduce the Court's freedom to intrigue. It also had the effect of raising women's political consciousness, even as it aroused real fear across the entire male political class (Hufton, 1992, p. 18). Some women began to demand total equality of rights with men. For Pauline Léon, for instance, it was obvious when war broke out that the women of Paris should be allowed to form a unit of the national guard to defend the capital. The request was, of course, ignored. But among some women an early feminism was taking root which would allow no distinctions in law between men and women. It fell to Olympe de Gouges, a butcher's daughter from Montauban, to express this most succinctly in her pamphlet on *The Rights of Women*, published in 1791. 'The principle of all sovereignty', she wrote, 'rests essentially with the nation, which is nothing but the union of woman and man.' As for the law, it 'must be the expression of the general will; all female and male citizens must contribute either personally or through their representatives to its formation.' And to men she threw down a resounding challenge. 'What gives you sovereign empire to oppress my sex? Your strength? Your talents? Observe the Creator in his wisdom; survey in all her grandeur that nature with which you seem to want to be in harmony, and give me, if you dare, an example of this tyrannical empire' (Levy, Applewhite and Johnson, 1979, pp. 89–90). Ideas of liberty and equality, intended as they were for men, could not but benefit women, too.

The hostility shown by many revolutionaries towards the idea of women as citizens was paralleled by an ambivalence towards France's colonial population. There had been a certain Enlightened opposition to the slave trade in the later eighteenth century, culminating in the founding of a reform club, the Amis des Noirs, in 1788. Yet the issue of slavery was little mentioned in the early months of the Revolution, when the deputies showed themselves to be narrowly French in their concerns. This may seem suprising, given the ideals which the revolutionaries set themselves. If 'all men are born and remain free and equal in rights', were not these rights to include those who were born into slavery, or those who were black? Or would an assault on the institution of slavery be interpreted as an attack on another of the Revolution's sacred causes, that of property? In fact, the proposals that were made were for the abolition of the slave trade on the Atlantic rather than for the freeing of those already enslaved. But events in the sugar islands rapidly forced the deputies' hands. The social fabric of Saint-Domingue and the other Caribbean islands was complicated by the fact that there were amongst the colonial population both slaves and freemen, negroes and mulattos, the free *hommes de couleur*; and the ringing proclamation of the Rights of Man in metropolitan France evoked an echo among both communities. In Saint-Domingue a political struggle rapidly developed between the white planters and the coloured community, with a violent uprising in October 1790 leading to brutal repression: the coloured leader, Ogé, was broken on the wheel in Le Cap. Reform followed only slowly, though some at least of the deputies, most notably Brissot, were outraged by the atrocities being committed in the name of France. In May 1791 the Assembly was moved to grant civil liberties to coloureds, but that did nothing to appease the slaves, who were as likely to be oppressed by the coloureds as by the French. In August of the same year the island was swept by a slave revolt that would last for twelve years and would make Toussaint-Louverture the first black liberation leader in history. Again France responded, if only to help defeat the British and

Spanish forces who were now threatening France's colonies in the Caribbean. In July 1793, on a motion of the *abbé* Grégoire, all subsidies to the slave trade were withdrawn. In October the commissioner sent out from the Convention, Sonthonax, anxious to attract blacks to fight for France, announced the end of slavery throughout Saint-Domingue; and early in the following year Paris responded by abolishing it in all French colonies. The curious thing, perhaps, is that the French response was so slow and so grudging. For if Brissot, Clavière, Condorcet and a handful of like-minded deputies showed a consistent interest in the issue of slavery, many others – including many leading radicals – showed little such concern. After the end of the Constituent Assembly, Yves Benot notes that neither Robespierre nor the Jacobin Club had anything to say on the colonial issue; Marat likewise remained silent (Benot, 1988, p. 101).

The French Revolution placed a high value on service, especially service to the state, and this is largely reflected in its social priorities. Those who gained most included those groups whose commitment to the regime was strongest – like lawyers, state officials, local administrators, and, increasingly, the military. Education, too, was given high priority, albeit within the limits imposed by an uncertain budget. Education had clear ideological implications and was too sensitive a matter to be left to the priests and teaching orders of the *ancien régime*, who, it was widely assumed, would inculcate Christian values and pave the way for the return of royalism. Hence responsibility for the enlightenment of its citizens must rest with the state. It was the state which organized national libraries and created a great national art gallery in the Louvre. And it was the state which, increasingly, assumed responsibility for schooling. Lay education – soon to be classed among the most valued of republican institutions – was demanded at all levels. At the highest level of excellence the Directory founded the first of the *grandes écoles* in Paris, the Ecole Normale Supérieure and the Polytechnique, schools which regarded service to the state as the most noble of callings and which were to preach the value of public service to generations of Frenchmen. But it was around primary schooling that the republicans debated most hotly, seeing this as the area where young minds could be formed and where the innocent must be defended from the depredations of Catholic catechism. When large numbers of clerics refused to take the oath under the Civil Constitution, the existing fabric was in any case in tatters. But how could the monks and priests be replaced, given that there was no tradition of lay teaching or of secularized teacher training that could produce the large numbers of secular schoolmasters that the regime required. The Jacobin solution is to be found in the Lakanal Law of November 1794, which laid down that in every commune with more than one thousand inhabitants the Republic would establish a primary school for boys and girls and would employ *instituteurs* and *institutrices* recruited and examined within each district. In the context of 1794 the plan was, of course, utopian; it reflected the ambitions and energies of men like Lakanal rather than the economic capacities of the times. Yet throughout the years of the Directory, as Isser Woloch has shown, bits and pieces of the plan were resurrected and politicians repeatedly asked that a programme of lay primary education be implemented. The dream was not to be forgotten, however empty the Republic's rhetoric on the subject was shown to have been (Lucas, 1988, pp. 372–3).

Napoleon and the Revolution's social policy

In many areas of social policy the Revolution's achievement survived the overthrow of the Directory at Brumaire. For although Napoleon was eager to instil social order in France to buttress the political order, he was not a social reactionary and had little affection for the system of estates and corporate privilege which had been swept away. Rather he was an unashamed believer in meritocracy, and he sought to temper revolutionary ideals through the creation of a new and talented elite in French society. Outstanding public service, in administration or politics but especially in the army, would be rewarded, and in this way loyalty would be assured and the state itself would be strengthened. The political aim blended neatly with the social. New nobles were created (though their number was never large); military aides became marshals of France; trusted friends from the army could also hope to become prefects. Public servants saw their work recognized by the award of the *légion d'honneur*, while honours were also used to encourage science and invention. Even the Senate could be seen as something of a social institution: Louis Bergeron has described it as 'a sort of microcosm in which more than a hundred highest notabilities were concentrated' (Bergeron, 1981, p. 54). Once again talent was everything and birth counted for little: of his marshals, for instance, Ney was the son of a barrelmaker, Murat of an innkeeper. Nor were men of ability excluded from office by past political allegiances. The vast majority of those promoted by Napoleon had already held public office during the Revolution, and nearly seventy of those who became prefects had belonged to one or other of the revolutionary assemblies of the 1790s. As Bergeron rightly observes, what the Empire had done was not to revoke the social mobility of the Revolution but to confirm the promotion of an entire generation of men from middling origins and to include them among the elite of the land. Those who lost out were not the revolutionaries – even ex-Jacobins could find themselves rewarded – but those who had held high office in the last years of the monarchy (Bergeron, 1981, pp. 56–60).

What distinguished Napoleon's period of power was the clear primacy of authority, in economic and social matters as well as the political sphere, and at every level of society. The quest for social order was everywhere in evidence – in the meticulous codification of the law, in the tightening of administrative control, in the reorganization of the police. In the departments the new office of prefect strengthened the hand of central government at the expense of those elected by local people. In the armies the qualities of discipline and professionalism were again emphasized. Everywhere obedience and authority took precedence over individual liberties. So too, within the family, the Napoleonic code placed renewed emphasis on the role of the father and husband. Though some of the gains of the Revolution remained intact – divorce was confirmed even where there was no evidence of adultery, for example, and both partners could continue to own individual property within a marriage – many of the more libertarian reforms were now reversed. Under the Code Napoléon parental authority was again stressed over children, and the authority of husbands over their wives; the rights of illegitimate children were discouraged, the grounds for divorce tightened, and the equal division of property abolished. These changes had considerable normative importance, since they underlined the message that even in microcosm society was clearly structured, with an authority figure at the apex of the pyramid. The political significance of that message was scarcely veiled.

This desire to stamp order on French society after the upheaval of the revolutionary years extended also to matters of religion. Large sections of the peasantry had never come to terms with the anti-clericalism of the Republic, and Napoleon needed their support, both as food producers and as soldiers. He may have had little religious faith of his own, but he understood fully its value to others and its implications for the governance of the country; and a compliant Church provided valuable opportunities for surveillance and control. His pact with Rome – the Concordat of 1801 – was a politically inspired move which served his interests well. Little was conceded. Catholicism was declared, quite factually, to be 'the religion of the great majority of the citizens'; new bishops were to be selected by the First Consul, not by the Pope; and the Church was subjected to strict policing and governmental regulation. In return the Pope regained spiritual control of the richest state in Christendom. But the triumph was Napoleon's. While building on the Revolution's anti-clerical achievement, he had guaranteed a degree of political stability which the revolutionaries had forfeited by their long-standing quarrel with Rome. And he had taken an important step in a much larger process, that of extending the imperium of the state over the social fabric as well as the body politic. Religion would resume its traditional social function, so rudely challenged by the Revolution, of helping to cement the social order and act as a bulwark to the authority of government.

5

War

On 20 April 1792 the Legislative Assembly voted to declare war on Austria, or, as the deputies preferred to express it, on the 'King of Hungary and Bohemia'. It was a momentous decision, and one that would affect the character of the Revolution for the rest of the decade. For the war was not to be, as contemporaries assumed, short, decisive and victorious. The condition of French arms would not permit of easy victory, and the first engagements administered a cruel shock as their armies were driven back and French territory was threatened. But even once victories began to be won and the morale of the French troops was restored, there was little hope of a quick conclusion to hostilities. The Assembly's narrowly defined war aims proved to be hopelessly unrealistic. The French nation, the Assembly declared, was taking up arms only in defence of its liberty and its independence; it had no quarrel with the other peoples of Europe. It even offered to adopt in advance 'all foreigners who, abjuring the cause of her enemies, come to range themselves under her banners and devote their efforts to the defence of her liberty' (Hardman, 1981, p. 141). This was a generous offer, an affirmation of the Assembly's belief in the brotherhood of man. It accepted the spirit of the constitution, which stated that France should never 'undertake any war with a view to making conquests'. But once the war was declared such sentiments quickly gave way to a more brutal and exclusive nationalism. Within a year France would be at war with most of the crowned heads of Europe; and by 1793 the very fact of being a foreign national was sufficient to make one appear suspect. The war declared on 20 April would drag on for the rest of the decade until, under the Directory and the Consulate, it overshadowed all the other aims of the Revolution and became the principal objective of the state.

Reasons for war

Why did France declare war? Did the origins of the conflict lie, as some would have us believe, in ideology, in a clash between incompatible and antagonistic political systems? Was it the case that the French declaration of war was largely technical, that France was about to be invaded by the monarchies of Europe, fearful lest the corrosive ideas preached by the French Revolution undermine the political fabric of their own states? This was the view of many contemporaries, and most notably of the Girondin deputies in their pro-war speeches to the Assembly. They pointed to the *émigré* armies assembling in foreign capitals like Mainz and Koblenz, openly enjoying the protection of local rulers. They believed, rightly, that Marie-Antoinette was conspiring with her Austrian relatives and plotting the downfall of the Revolution: the public obloquy in which the young queen was widely held only confirmed the image of her as a traitor and a spy for a foreign power. Louis's endless vacillations did nothing to rebuild the image of the monarchy, and the King's flight to Varennes in the summer of 1791 further heightened French fears of a counter-revolutionary assault from across the Rhine. News of the King's arrest and humiliation evoked a hostile response from the monarchies of Europe. In England it helped to turn popular sentiment against the Revolution. And at Pillnitz the Emperor of Austria and the King of Prussia issued a joint declaration condemning the Revolution and inviting the other monarchies of Europe to join them in re-establishing order in France. For the princes and the *émigré* nobles it was the promise of armed intervention they were seeking, even though there was little chance in 1791 that others would throw in their lot with Leopold. As for the revolutionary leaders in Paris, many of them took the declaration at face value, as a threat to reimpose the Bourbons on the French people.

The war party was composed of several factions, including most of the Girondin group in the Assembly and the supporters of La Fayette. Their aims may have been widely divergent, but their short-lived alliance was a crucial boost for the cause of war. The Girondins were especially vocal in the anti-Austrian campaign. Foremost among them was Brissot, who argued passionately that war was not an option but a necessity for the French people. Like his Girondin colleagues, his language was infused with a belligerent nationalism, and it was nothing less than the sovereignty of the nation that was at issue. In December 1791 he told the Assembly that the time had come for 'a new crusade, a crusade for universal freedom' (Lefebvre, 1962, I, p. 217). In his *Discours sur la nécessité de déclarer la guerre* Brissot argued that war was necessary if the French were to establish their liberty on a firm foundation, that through war the people could purge the vices of despotism and rid themselves of those who were still a source of corruption. Besides, added Brissot, if France did not attack, other nations would think her weak; to be strong, the Revolution needed to impose itself through war (Ellery, 1915, p. 233). He saw war as a cause that would be popular not only with patriots at home but also among the peoples of Europe whom the French would liberate from tyranny. At home war would rally national sentiment behind the revolution and force an unwilling monarch to opt for a revolutionary programme and for revolutionary ministers. Abroad Brissot genuinely seems to have believed that war would not present France with any tangible dangers. For, he explained, with the optimism of the true extremist, French troops would be welcomed into Germany by the local people who would see them as the missionaries of a new order, bringing freedom in their knapsacks (Hampson, 1981, p. 5).

Others took up the same theme. Some, like the Swiss Clavière or the various Dutch exiles who pressed their opinions on Brissot, had clear personal reasons for championing war (Bosher, 1988, p. 160). Yet others spoke out of pure conviction. Gensonné, persuaded by Brissot's arguments, rallied the Diplomatic Committee to support for war against Austria and insisted that the Emperor should be asked to make his intentions clear. In particular, he should undertake not to attack the French nation, its constitution or its complete freedom to establish its chosen form of government (Stephens, 1892, I, p. 401). Warming to his theme, Vergniaud argued that the Revolution had aroused fear in all the monarchies of Europe, that it had given others an example of how despots could be toppled, and that it was only a matter of time before the despots counter-attacked. It was in France's interest, therefore, to surprise her enemies by taking the first step and proclaiming the declaration of war (Stephens, 1892, I, p. 276).

Not all agreed with this diagnosis. Robespierre, in particular, warned against too hasty a response to the provocations of kings and emperors, provocations which he saw as intended to weaken France by dissipating her energies in war when there were more important domestic battles to be fought. In two speeches delivered to the Jacobin Club in January 1792 Robespierre distanced himself from the Girondin enthusiasm for war and urged his colleagues to be cautious. It was doubtless a noble and selfless gesture for France to have promised to help others achieve their liberty, he argued, but it was a gesture that was fraught with perils. And these perils had to be recognized. He would, he said, be as eager as anyone to send an army into Brabant or to help the people of Liège, he would vie with Brissot in his enthusiasm for combat, but for one consideration. If France became embroiled in foreign adventures would not this benefit royalists and counter-revolutionaries at home? Was not this exactly what those most opposed to the Revolution – the *émigré* nobles, the aristocratic army officers, the Court, the

Queen – wanted the revolutionaries to do? The fact that these groups were braying loudly for war only strengthened Robespierre's suspicions. And he rapidly turned his fire on the Girondins, who, he said, were trying to use the mood of war to distract attention from their failings at home. Some – and Dumouriez's treachery several months later gave credence to this view – were already sold to the Court interest. Robespierre and those Jacobins who supported him were convinced that by declaring war France's leaders would be playing into the hands of their enemies (Stephens, 1892, II, p. 304).

In the spring of 1792 it was the Girondin view that prevailed, and Robespierre, like everyone else, closed ranks in support of the troops and the success of the armies. But were Brissot and his supporters right to assume that this was an ideological war, different in kind from the succession of conflicts which had pitted France against Austria, Prussia and Britain throughout the eighteenth century? T. C. W. Blanning thinks that there is little reason to believe so. Eighteenth-century governments saw war and diplomacy in terms of imperial conquest and dynastic interest. They went to war when they believed that they could win, when the other side seemed vulnerable: this could be because it was financially weak or militarily depleted, because the succession was contested or because its interests were engaged elsewhere. They fought to obtain limited advantages, colonies or tracts of disputed land; they did not go to war in order to destroy the political system of the other side. And seen from the vantage point of Berlin or Vienna, why should these considerations have changed? If Austria or Prussia were attracted by the possibilities of a war with France, was it not because they sensed that the Revolution had reduced France's military capacity by destroying the military high command and deepening the fiscal crisis of the 1780s? And if they held back, was it not for equally strategic reasons, that during this period their real interests were concentrated elsewhere, on the job of partitioning Poland? Britain, too, might be expected to view the state of France's defences with a pragmatic rather than an ideological eye. For their last conflict, in America, had ended in British concessions and that most unusual outcome, a French naval victory at Yorktown. A new war, at a time when French attention was concentrated elsewhere, might serve to regain the French sugar islands and to re-establish British control of the seas.

There is little evidence to support the view that Leopold was driven by anti-revolutionary enthusiasm to seek a war with France. On the contrary, we know that he sympathized with some at least of France's proposed reforms, and if the Duke of Brunswick subsequently gave the Austrian campaign an ideological justification through his famous manifesto, it was one that he soon came to regret. Leopold's view was that the French were there for the taking: the Austrians even talked of a walk-over, of the French giving up without a fight. The Prussians shared this optimism, believing that France could be defeated within two months. They had, they believed, nothing to lose (Blanning, 1986, p. 116). But what of the revolutionaries themselves? Despite their ideological rhetoric, Blanning concludes that France's own calculations were no less pragmatic. If the war party in the Assembly used political language, it was only because by 1792 it had become almost obligatory to justify policy in political terms. He points to continuities which marked French foreign policy throughout the eighteenth century, and from which revolutionary opinion was not immune – notably a marked Anglophobia on the one hand, and Austrophobia on the other. Foreign policy after 1789 was following in a well marked furrow, and since it was now being made and debated in the full glare of publicity which surrounded every debate in the Assembly, it had little option but to take account of opinion in the country. Besides, the revolutionaries were influenced by the most pragmatic consideration of all, the fact that they believed they were well placed to win. They were convinced that the French people were invincible when faced with monarchs and tyrants; and the ease with which they had annexed Avignon in 1790 added to their false sense of security. Like their opponents they calculated that defeat was unthinkable and that victory could be cheaply won.

The course of the war

That calculation proved to be terribly wrong. The French had indeed taken the Austrians by surprise, but they did nothing to capitalize on their advantage. Early campaigning was both badly coordinated and desperately unsuccessful. Dumouriez, in effective charge of military strategy, attempted to isolate the Austrians and annex Belgium, hoping to score quick and emphatic victories along the northern frontier. He failed, the campaign turning into an undignified mixture of confusion, indiscipline and defeat. Of the generals sent into action only Custine enjoyed any success (he captured the fortress of Porrentruy); elsewhere armies surrendered territorial advantage or pulled back without engaging the enemy. Everywhere there was a sense of failure, combined with the increasingly political charge that the military were being deliberately undermined. Officers were accused of incompetence and treason and lost the confidence of their regiments. In one case, after ordering his men to retreat, General Dillon was murdered in the streets of Lille. Morale slumped as the military campaign was increasingly engulfed in political faction fighting. In consequence, the early advantage which the French enjoyed was soon squandered. By early July the war was extended when France opened hostilities against Prussia; on 11 July the *patrie* was declared *en danger*, a move which heralded new restrictions on the civilian population; and during August French territory was invaded from both the north and the east. A war that had been declared with such innocent bravado a few months before seemed increasingly likely to turn into a national catastrophe.

By the end of 1792, however, French fortunes had staged a quite spectacular resurgence. Morale was suddenly restored as armies which had become conditioned to expect defeat now began to taste victory. The turning-point came at Valmy on 20 September, where the armies of Dumouriez and Kellermann massed their artillery to defeat a Prussian army which would otherwise have had France, and possibly Paris, at its mercy. It was a victory which was as unexpected as it was crucial: Valmy

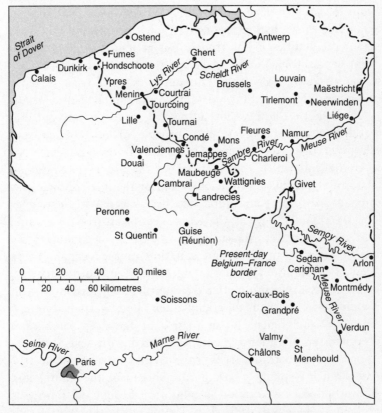

Figure 7 The campaigns of the Armée du Nord, 1792–1794
Source: J. A. Lynn, *The Bayonets of the Republic: Motivation and Tactics in the Army of Revolutionary France, 1791–94* (University of Illinois Press, 1984).

'turned back the foreign invasion and saved the new regime in France' (Scott, 1978, p. 172). It also heralded a rapid succession of important victories. By the end of September General Montesquiou had taken Savoy and Nice; by the end of October Custine had annexed the Rhineland, including the cities of Frankfurt and Mainz; and at the end of October Dumouriez led an army of 40,000 men against Belgium. On 6 November this force engaged the Austrians at Jemappes, winning a second famous battle. As Scott explains, the importance of Jemappes was in many ways far greater than Valmy. For Valmy had been won by the artillery, with little hand-to-hand fighting. It contained more than an element of good fortune and told little about the abilities of the troops. But at Jemappes they had to fight hard and resolutely, withstanding attack after attack; they had proved themselves, as Dumouriez himself recognised, in the most difficult of all contexts, that of a pitched battle (Scott, 1978, p. 174). The French had proved, to the enemy but also to themselves, that they were capable of the courage and discipline that were called for in an infantry engagement.

In the winter of 1792 it was easy for the French to be carried away by the enthusiasm of victory and by the force of their own propaganda. The Convention had been elected in September and the republic formed; the King was put on trial for his life; and the September Massacres were a timely reminder of the extent of popular panic and agitation in the capital. There seemed to be little that the infant republic could not achieve. Abroad, the Convention offered 'fraternity and assistance' to all peoples who wished to regain their liberty, and the new Girondin government began to talk of the need for natural frontiers, an ambition which they shared with several generations of Bourbon monarchs. In November Brissot wrote that 'the French Republic's only border should be the Rhine', and he warned that 'we cannot be calm until Europe, all Europe is in flames' (Lefebvre, 1962, I, p. 274). During the months that followed Savoy and Nice were incorporated in the French Republic, and Belgium and the Rhineland effectively annexed, while the old bishopric of Basle became the French department of Mont-Terrible. Confident of its armies, the Republic was coming more and more to adopt a nationalist and imperialistic approach to conquest, an approach which consolidated Austrian and Prussian opposition and which drew other nations into the war. In London Pitt had held to a position of neutrality for as long as he could, but the execution of Louis created an upsurge of anti-French feeling in England, and French aggression in Belgium affected a region where Britain had traditional friendships and alliances. The invasion of Belgium, the threat to Holland and the opening up of the Scheldt to shipping all contributed to a breakdown in relations. On 1 February the Convention pre-empted any British move by itself declaring war, and it followed this on 7 March with a declaration of war on Spain. By the spring of 1793 France was at war with a First Coalition that included most of the great powers of western Europe.

The euphoria created by Valmy and Jemappes soon evaporated as the French suffered reverses on all fronts. In March Dumouriez met with serious defeat at Neerwinden, after which he was forced to abandon any ambitions on Holland and fall back on Liège. Worse still was to follow, however, as Dumouriez tried to place the blame for his defeat on the War Department and made his own political settlement with the Austrians. Without any authority from Paris, he ordered the closure of Jacobin clubs and restored plate to Belgian churches, and signed an armistice with the enemy which involved the surrender of several forts along the northern frontier (Sutherland, 1985, p. 168). When he went further and tried to turn his army against the Republic in defence of the now discredited constitution of 1791, the soldiers refused to follow him and Dumouriez emigrated. But the damage inflicted on French morale was incalculable. In the north the Austrians took advantage of French discomfiture and crossed the frontier, laying siege to several towns, including Valenciennes. In the east the Prussians cut off a French army at Mainz. And in the Pyrenees the Spanish forces counter-attacked, taking a number of villages on the French side of the border and advancing on Perpignan itself.

The military situation by the summer of 1793 was again desperate, made worse by the fact that troops were pinned down in the West facing the insurgents of the Vendée. In the eyes of many the Girondin administration stood condemned by charges of military incompetence and connivance in treason.

It was during the months of the Jacobin Republic that France's military fortunes were once again transformed and the country liberated from foreign armies. This was the period when the affairs of the army came increasingly under the control of the Committee of Public Safety, and most especially of the member of that committee most interested in war, Lazare Carnot. In the south west the Spaniards were driven out of the Pyrénées-orien-tales and the war taken on to Spanish soil. And in the north the republican troops showed that they could take on and defeat the best armies in Europe. On 26 June the Austrians were routed at Fleurus and the French once again found themselves in a position to attack Belgium. Little over a week later the armies of Pichegru and Jourdan were poised to take Brussels and Antwerp; the threat to northern France had disappeared. And with both the Prussians and the Austrians seeking peace – Prussia was by now far more interested in the spoils which seemed to beckon in Poland – the First Coalition was effectively over. The key settlement was the Treaty of Basel, signed with Prussia on 5 April 1795, which split the somewhat rickety alliance of Prussia with Austria and recog-nized French claims to the left bank of the Rhine. This in turn allowed the French government to impose its own terms on the Dutch in the Treaty of The Hague and to prepare for the permanent annexation of Belgium. Spain made peace two months later.

Victory

After the summer of 1794 France was no longer under threat of invasion and the republic's first war aim, to save the *patrie en danger*, had been achieved. Crucially, too, she no longer faced the combined might of Austria and Prussia to the east;

Prussia had no interest in resuming hostilities, and Austria was now allied only to a sprinkling of German electorates. But there remained the problem of Britain which, despite the treaties with Prussia, Holland and Spain, was still at war and sought to open up a new front in Brittany, aided, the British hoped, by Puisaye and a *chouan* army. The result, the Quiberon landing of June 1795, was a disaster for Britain, as Hoche cut off the British and their allies at the foot of the Quiberon Peninsula and drove them into the sea. But the French government took the affair seriously, and it hardened French attitudes. In this second phase of the war there was, however, one important difference from the campaigns of 1793 and 1794. The war over which the Thermidorians and the Directory presided was not a war to save France from its enemies, to defend a revolution endangered by its ideological opponents. There was little about it, indeed, that could be described as ideological. It was a straightforward war of conquest unleashed by the Revolution in order to build on previous gains and to secure food and other supplies from continental Europe. France's military ambitions appeared limitless. By 1797 she had set up a series of buffer states to protect her military conquests, like the Batavian Republic in Holland and the Helvetic Republic in Switzerland; French forces had even committed the ultimate outrage of entering Rome. At Campio-Formio in October the Austrians were forced to accept Bonaparte's terms and northern Italy lay at the mercy of the French.

Yet victory brought its own problems. The Directory was unpopular at home, being widely regarded as bureaucratic, corrupt and oppressive, while abroad the armies won famous victories and encapsulated everything that was most glorious and patriotic in the revolutionary dream. The Directors viewed the war as a means of preserving morale and deflecting attention from domestic failures; but the military high command were becoming ever more independent and increasingly contemptuous of their political masters. Bonaparte was uniquely well placed to distance himself from the Directory. As commander-in-chief in Italy he enjoyed rare economic freedom as a result of the fruits of plunder and carefully massaged his own propaganda in a succession of army newspapers. In *La France vue de l'Armée de l'Italie*, for instance, Frenchmen at home as well as soldiers in the field could read of Bonaparte as a moral purist who contrasted nobly with the corruption of all around him: 'I have seen kings at my feet', he wrote in 1797, 'I could have had fifty millions in my coffers, I could have laid claim to a variety of things, but I am a French citizen, I am the chief general of the Great Nation; I know that posterity will do me justice' (Tulard, 1985, p. 61). In practice, however, he saw himself as far more than a general of the Great Nation since he could depend on the loyalty of his men, even when he acted in defiance of orders from Paris. By 1797 it was Bonaparte, not the Directors, who took the essential political decisions in northern Italy. It was he who declared war on Venice, he who determined the terms of Campio-Formio, he who made Lombardy into the Cisalpine Republic and seized Genoa as an outlet to the sea. His prestige served to diminish the reputation of the politicians and built the springboard from which he would challenge for power at Brumaire.

Brumaire, the conquest of the political arm of government by the military, changed the nature of revolutionary government and arguably heralded the end of the Revolution itself. It was the most extreme example during the revolutionary decade of the impact of war on France's political institutions. But it should not be thought of as the only example. Ever since the declaration of the first hostilities in 1792, war had had a powerful impact on revolutionary France, altering national priorities and restricting the choices which France's leaders enjoyed. Even revolutionary ideology was altered, the generous universalist message of 1789 giving way to a much more patriotic and exclusive view of France. Whereas the National Assembly had welcomed Paine, Anacharsis Cloots and all other 'citizens of the world' to make common cause with France, the declaration of war turned these men into enemies, slaves of tyrants and potential spies. Frenchmen alone had a monopoly of those qualities which constituted republican virtue. And, though it was France which in every case declared war, republicans had little difficulty in persuading themselves that it was they, their institutions and their values, which were under attack. Norman Hampson has discussed the duality implicit in the term *patrie* and shown how the two meanings fused in the wake of France's declaration of war. 'The new France, in which citizens were supposed to identify themselves with the community whose legislators, administrators, judges and priests they elected, could only survive if it protected itself against foreign invasion' (Lucas, 1988, p. 132). While the country remained at war the revolutionaries would appeal to the passion of patriotism, to the defence of the territory of France. But they were also appealing for the survival of virtue, of the *patrie* in the republican sense.

Historians have long argued about the part played by the war in the demise of revolutionary liberalism. Some see the denial of liberalism as central to a republican ideology that was being expressed long before the suspension of the King. They date the authoritarian instincts of the revolutionaries to the period of constitutional monarchy, to the idea that sovereignty lay in the people and that it could not be divided or alienated. The essence of the Republic, in Pierre Nora's view, was already in place by June of 1789, when the Estates-General had accepted their new role as a national assembly (Furet and Ozouf, 1988, p. 832). Others, however, have taken a less ideological view of the republic and have accepted that the move towards authoritarian government had its roots in the day-to-day problems of food supply, counter-revolution and war. Of course the Paris sections called vehemently for terror as a weapon to be used against hoarders and traitors. Royalist uprisings and the machinations of refractory priests added urgency to their call. But many would argue that it was the war, and the needs of the troops on the frontiers, which guaranteed the failure of moderation. For war bred both fear and envy. Fear of defeat, fear of bloody reprisals, fear of the aristocrats and royalists who were the known enemies of the new order, fear of a return to the Bourbons; these were powerful arguments in the cause of greater control and centralization. In Paris, it was, after all, fear of the bloody aftermath of military defeat which had sparked the September Massacres in the city's prisons. But war and the sacrifices of war also created a politics of envy – envy of those who tried to avoid service, who continued to trade and make profits while others were offering their lives to the *patrie*. The thought that some were escaping their responsibilities and continuing to accumulate wealth did not affect only the poor. It also helped cement the resolve of patriots and Jacobins to impose sacrifices equally on all, a resolve which led to an insistence on public duty, to increased surveillance, and ultimately to terror.

Effects of military reform

In a country at war, it was argued, the army demanded that civilians be seen to make sacrifices, that the soldiers should not be left to bear the entire burden of war. That was especially true in a revolutionary society where they were citizens, men with rights and political opinions of their own. They were angered when pensions were not paid to their wives and dependants, they demanded vengeance when their food rations were left to rot by corrupt contractors. In 1789 soldiers in Paris had joined the crowds on the Place de la Bastille to combat tyranny; and at Nancy in 1790 they had mutinied against their own officers to demand better pay and conditions. Increasingly, indeed, the revolutionaries found themselves forced to put their trust in the virtues of the ordinary soldier, his sense of duty, of service, of essential fairness; for they could not trust the officers they inherited from the royal army of the 1780s. Since the Ségur Ordinance of 1781 the law had insisted that all officers must be nobles, men cut off by their upbringing, their military education and their sense of privilege from the men they commanded. Often the sons and younger brothers of *émigrés*, they had little reason to love the Revolution: they had taken an oath of personal loyalty to the King, and most of them knew nothing of the sovereignty of the people. When faced with a choice between serving a revolution from which they felt increasingly alienated and serving their king in exile, many of them chose to resign their commissions and pass into emigration. This was especially true after Louis's flight to Varennes: between mid-September and the beginning of December 1791 some 2,160 officers chose to emigrate (Scott, 1978, pp. 106–8). The government had little reason to believe that it could trust those who remained.

The revolutionaries found new officers from within the ranks of the army itself, from the many corporals and sergeants who had distinguished themselves in the wars of the late eighteenth century but who could have nurtured no thoughts of promotion in the royal regiments. Promotion was now based on talent, not on birth, an attack on established hierarchies within the most hierarchical of all the institutions of the state. It also helped create a very different kind of army, where officers talked the same language as their men and where discipline was based more on consent and mutual respect. Where the former noble commanders remained in post – and many of them did, right through the Jacobin republic – they had to justify their actions, both to their men and to the deputies on mission and political *commissaires* who accompanied the armies. As citizens, soldiers had new and unparalleled political rights (Bertaud, 1988). In 1793 and 1794 they were encouraged to sing patriotic songs, read radical newspapers and attend meetings of local Jacobin clubs in the towns where they were garrisoned. They could also denounce their own officers if they felt that they were being betrayed or if poor tactics led to unnecessary losses. On their arrival with the Army of the Rhine, Saint-Just and Le Bas issued a proclamation which appealed directly to the troops. Victory could be obtained only if everyone were to pull together and traitors were exposed. 'If there are amongst you', they told the men, 'traitors or men indifferent to the people's cause, we bring the sword that shall strike them. Soldiers! We have come to avenge you and bring you leaders who will conduct you to victory. We are resolved to seek out merit, to reward and promote it and to track down every crime, whoever may have committed it' (Hampson, 1991, p. 146). It could be a painful form of political education. In the north alone three of the army's generals would be guillotined within a single year.

If the Revolution had to find new officers, it also had to find new men to fill the ranks, men who would be proud to serve a cause in which they believed. For the morale of the old line army was poor. Too often men joined in the eighteenth century because they saw no alternative to service, no place for them-selves in civilian society. Often they were the younger sons of poor peasants who had no hope of finding land of their own and were condemned to a marginal existence on the fringes of village life. Some joined the army as a means of escape, whether from the law after some youthful escapade or from home after a family row. Many were press-ganged into service. And once in the army discipline was maintained by harsh and brutal methods which enforced submission rather than creating any bonds of loyalty or trust. The revolutionaries were convinced that such an army was poorly suited to the tasks before it, and the high incidence of mutiny and desertion in the early months of the Revolution meant that new soldiers had to be found quickly. But how was this to be done? In 1791 and 1792 the government still fondly believed that the regiments could be filled by a call for volunteers, but that hope rapidly faded. And when the war started, early losses and tactics which demanded large numbers of infantrymen produced a serious manpower shortage. From the spring of 1793 quotas were set which local communities were expected to meet, and by August of that year – the month of the famous *levée en masse* – Paris insisted that ballots be used to determine which of the young men of each commune would leave for the regiments. The *levée en masse* also forbade the purchase of replacements to serve in one's place; for the first time an attempt was being made to compel all those designated – even those who were rich or well connected – to perform the military service that was implicit in citizenship.

A war economy

If the armies required men, they also required guaranteed sources of supply, especially during the early months of the war when French troops were pinned back on French soil. This need was urgent: the Revolution was well aware that ill-fed troops would turn to looting and pillage to fill their bellies, and that pillage would in turn lead to disaffection and disorder in the ranks. With thousands of men deployed within local regions of the country, moreover, it was scarcely realistic to depend on local farmers or on the local market to provide for their needs. France was forced to adopt an ever greater measure of economic control. The commitment to the free market had to be amended to allow for the huge scale of requisitions which the armies required. Farmers were compelled to sell their produce at their local market, where, under the Jacobins, prices were fixed by the Law of the General Maximum. Army contractors were authorized to make bulk purchases, often in the face of opposition from local people. Whole regions were designated as supply zones from which vital supplies of grain, flour, meat, vegetables and wine could be taken for the use of the military. And we know that in periods of extreme shortage deputies on mission even allowed the army to pay prices above the level of the maximum, breaking the law to ensure that the troops did not starve. Increasingly, indeed, the Revolution was moving towards a war economy, which necessarily had different priorities from those that prevailed in peace time. Feeding the troops and maintaining some minimum sense of well-being in the armies became, unavoidably, one of the highest priorities of the state.

It was not just food that had to be requisitioned. Economic controls were rapidly applied to other products, too, as contractors and commissioners sought to ensure that the armies were given the resources they needed to fight effectively for France. They needed to be clothed as well as fed, at a time when the country did not have the industrial infrastructure to provide uniforms for several hundred thousand men. In the early days the solutions adopted were basic, even rather primitive, with communes ordered to provide a complete uniform for every man they raised for the war effort. But by 1793 such hand-to-mouth solutions were patently inadequate to the task in hand, and the government was forced to order fixed quotas of jackets, trousers and shirts from the seamstresses of Paris and other cities. When Bouchotte was at the Ministry of War, much of the work was channelled through public workshops set up in the Paris sections, which gave the government a greater measure of leverage and control. But throughout the Revolution the complaints continued to flow in, and even in Year VII it was clear that the clothing industry, based on small domestic units, could cope only with the greatest difficulty. The supply of boots was equally problematic, since it relied on the organization of thousands of *cordonniers* and *sabotiers*, small-scale neighbourhood craftsmen who now found themselves engaged by government contractors. In Year II Bouchotte ordered that every shoemaker in France must supply a fixed quota of boots for the army proportionate to the number of the men he employed; there was even a period of crisis during the winter of 1793–4 when shoemakers were allowed to work only for the army (Forrest, 1990, pp. 140–1). And yet the problem remained intense. In *ventôse* of Year II Celliez wrote from the north that the shortage of footwear was causing outrage among the men of the Armée du Nord. 'Most of them still go barefoot, they do not even have clogs; there are angry murmurs in the ranks, and they are afraid that they will still be in this state when the campaigning season begins' (Soboul, 1959, p. 159).

Food, clothing and footwear posed major problems for army suppliers, problems that were symptomatic of a more general crisis. Soldiers needed arms and powder, tents and blankets; and too often they went short. If they fought with pikes, the symbol of republican *élan*, it was in response to shortage and necessity, whatever the claims of the politicians. Collot d'Herbois, in September 1793, issued a memorable clarion call: 'Isn't it the bayonet, cold steel, that makes the French superior to the slaves of tyrants?' (Bertaud, 1989, p. 155). But he was only putting a brave face on a desperate situation. The Revolution did have state armouries to manufacture firearms, but they were never enough to satisfy the needs of a country at war. Guns had to be mended, too: in the hinterland of the larger armies gunsmiths, locksmiths and metalworkers were requisitioned by the republic to man emergency repair depots for the military. Families were asked to collect saltpetre in their cellars to help overcome a shortage of powder that was putting the whole war effort at risk. Firewood was an eternal problem, especially during the winter months in the mountains of northern Italy: whole woods had to be requisitioned if soldiers were not to freeze to death. And even if all these essentials were available, the armies still had to move them to the front, a huge exercise in military transport. Again, their own resources could seldom cope, and the government was forced to requisition a rich variety of carts and wagons from local farmers and foresters. Livestock were requisitioned too, from horses and oxen to mules and donkeys, placing an even greater burden on the poorer peasants who needed their animals for ploughing the fields, harvesting the crops, and also, vitally, for manure for the soil. When added to the surrender of their sons to the recruiting sergeant, the loss of their animals could place a dreadful burden on an already strained rural economy.

A war economy had little time for laissez-faire economics, and the liberal economic principles of 1789 were soon sacrificed to short-term needs. As the war was extended, so the Revolution passed more and more laws regulating trade and enforcing price controls, hoping by these means to force producers to sell and to curb the growing black economy. These controls also had a moral aspect: with so many young men being asked to serve the Republic in war, the *sans-culottes* and the more radical Jacobins believed that those lucky enough to escape active service should be prevented from profiteering at the expense of their fellow-citizens. Profits became an object of suspicion, and private interest was contrasted with the interest of the public, of the community at large. There were, of course, profits to be made, especially by army contractors and those able to exploit the economies of the states the French troops invaded. Success in the continental war opened up new markets for French goods. But after Britain's entry into the war, the normal import-export trade of France was undermined, and protectionism could be presented as the only viable way of ensuring that the citizenry would eat. The extension of the war to the Atlantic seaboard and the sinking of merchantmen by British warships killed off much of France's colonial and American trade, condemning France's Atlantic ports to severe recession and forcing the Revolution to depend far more on its own economic resources (Forrest and Jones, 1991, pp. 40–1).

Whether the economic results of war are interpreted as being wholly bad depends largely on the political viewpoint of the interpreter. For Marxist historians such as Albert Soboul war was the catalyst that enabled the Committee of Public Safety to move towards a controlled economy, which in turn helped lay the foundations of a fairer and more equal society. The committee sought to mobilize the whole of French society in this enterprise: and for the first time scientific research was put at the service of national defence. The whole approach is presented as being progressive and opposed to engrained privilege (Soboul, 1974, pp. 350–1). Economic liberals, on the other hand, are in no doubt that the overall balance sheet is negative, that the controls which the war made possible destroyed many of the early gains of the revolutionary period. Florin Aftalion puts this case with considerable vigour. After acknowledging that measures against gilds and corporations had helped to free trade from eighteenth-century restrictions, he sees the war as a turning-point in the economic history of the revolutionary decade. 'The protectionist tradition, which the Revolution might well have broken with, was in fact definitively established in this period, and was to last, with incalculably destructive consequences, up until the present time' (Aftalion, 1990, p. 193).

That the war had important consequences for the internal policies of the Revolution there can be little doubt. But just as important was its effect on the image which foreigners had of

France and its government. Initial reactions to the Revolution, at least among liberals, had often been highly favourable: in Holland, Britain, Switzerland and many of the German states the most advanced thinkers of the day had been among the most passionate advocates of revolutionary France. But the practical experience of war made many of them reconsider their initial enthusiasm. As the French armies surged across Europe it became increasingly evident that *pays ennemis* and *pays conquis* could expect little generosity from France. They were made to serve French national interests, and were annexed to France as additional departments (like Belgium) or formed into sister republics (like the Batavian or Helvetic republics) more or less at the whim of Paris. The French drew up new national boundaries; they proclaimed their need to establish national frontiers; and they claimed the right to impose political institutions on the states they conquered. The cause of liberty and self-determination had rapidly been forgotten; France was committed, it seemed, to far more selfish aims like national security and diplomatic convenience.

Besides, all the reforms that were brought by the French armies to the peoples of Europe were brought by occupation and conquest. It was only natural that Belgians, Italians and Germans should interpret their national interests rather differently from the interpretation placed upon it in Paris. And the memory of French occupation was both recent and highly unpleasant. French armies were ordered to live off the lands they occupied; indeed, the main purpose of annexations was often not the liberation of peoples suffering under tyranny but the acquisition of food and supplies for the military. On 18 September 1793 the Committee of Public Safety ordered commanders to find, as far as was possible, all the food, clothing, arms and equipment they needed in the territories they occupied. And in May of the following year four *agences de commerce* were set up with precise instructions to evacuate essential materials from occupied lands, not only objects of strategic importance for the war, but also works of art and national treasures. The effects could be devastating. In Belgium, for instance, half the grain harvest was requisitioned in 1795 to feed French troops. And that was the price which local people were expected to pay in official requisitions. They also had to cope with the other face of occupation, the costs exacted by an army of occupation. For like all eighteenth-century armies, the French could treat the local population with a cavalier brutality, seeing booty and plunder as their natural desserts in a continent at war. Fields were regularly stripped of crops, and farmers forced to part with their carts, horses, cattle, bedding and kitchen utensils. Despite occasional purges like that enforced by Saint-Just on the Rhine, there was little systematic attempt by the French to stamp out pillage. Local people had little choice but to tolerate such depredations; but they did not need to pretend that they enjoyed being liberated by the French, or that they had much affection for the Revolution in whose name that liberation was carried out (Furet and Ozouf, 1988, pp. 146–55).

The war took much of the idealism out of the Revolution, however hard the generals tried to instil political fervour into their troops. By 1795 – and even in large measure before – the revolutionary wars had become wars of conquest, fought to gain territorial advantage, and fought by armies that regarded themselves, first and foremost, as professional soldiers. And the cost to the Revolution was huge. The expense of fighting on such a scale and on so many different frontiers pushed France further down the road to inflation and economic coercion. It helped promote the case for terror and political intolerance. And by consuming so much of the government's time and resources, it prevented other revolutionary ambitions from being pursued and achieved. The war, in other words, distorted the Revolution and turned it away from its original goals. In that respect it may be said to have had much in common with counter-revolution which, in different guises, dogged the revolutionaries throughout the 1790s.

6

Opposition

The men of 1789 had entertained hopes of a new France based on ideals of liberty and equality before the law. They had dreamt of a country liberated from monarchical absolutism, untrammeled by clerical authority and seigneurial power. Revolutionary order was seen as liberty, as the freeing of the people of France from their traditional oppressors. Frenchmen were citizens, not subjects; and large numbers of them were invited to participate in the political process, through elections, political debate, newspaper readership, or the membership of clubs. But already in 1789 there were those – bishops and abbots, nobles and courtiers – who saw little in the new order for them and who sought refuge in emigration. The officer corps of the army, as we have seen, was rapidly decimated; and the King's abortive flight to Varennes in 1791 served to convince many others that they had no future in revolutionary France. For royalists, indeed, the choice seemed stark: either to obey their government or to follow the dictates of their conscience and remain loyal to their king. Many found the prescriptions of constitutional monarchy difficult to tolerate; and the decision to declare France a republic in 1792 proved the last straw. For others it was the threat to social hierarchy which turned them against the Revolution, their realization that from the outset the Revolution was opposed to nobility and intolerant of privilege. Many of them chose the road to Turin or Milan, London or Madrid, where they tried to recreate the court society that had once been theirs. Some among them would join royalist armies and fight for the restoration of monarchical institutions. They were the true counter-revolutionaries, those who were opposed to the very principles on which the Revolution was based. Unlike later emigrants, few were attracted by either the Directory or the Napoleonic years. Their return, if ever they did return, would generally be delayed until after the Bourbon restoration in 1814.

The counter-revolution

Just as the Revolution had its theorists and intellectual defenders, so did the counter-revolution. Most wrote from exile, having fled from France at some time between 1789 and 1792. The most famous of them was Jacques Mallet du Pan, whose *Considérations sur la Révolution de France*, published in Brussels in 1793, attacked the very notion of a social revolution as endangering order and turning the country over to mob rule. Outraged royalists like Rivarol placed their considerable journalistic talents at the service of the King, parodying the achievements of the revolutionaries and subjecting the National Assembly to the most savage and effective satire. Others, like the *abbé* Royou, played a more tactical game, seeking to woo a larger readership to their papers by preaching a more moderate form of royalism and a deeply conservative vision of Catholicism (Chisick, 1992, p. 63). Indeed, many of the royalist publicists of the period chose to link the attack on monarchy to the attack on the Church, portraying both as wicked and dangerous routes to anarchy. Most prominent among them was probably the *abbé* Barruel, who not only rejected the Civil Constitution of the Clergy – a predictable line of attack – but went on to attack the philosophy of individualism on which all of revolutionary thinking was based. Barruel berated the Revolution for its vision of the state as the coming together of

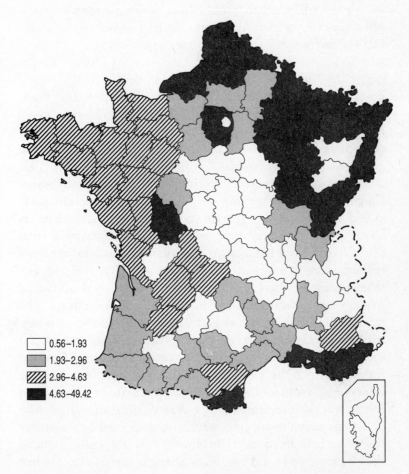

Figure 8 Numbers of *émigrés* per 1,000 inhabitants, by department
Source: D. Greer, *The Incidence of the Emigration during the French Revolution* (Harvard University Press, 1951).

individual interests. He preferred, in the best traditions of the *ancien régime*, to see it in corporate terms. As Jacques Godechot has remarked, for Barruel the state 'is formed of a whole series of families: the nation is the gathering of all the families and the king is, as it were, the *paterfamilias* of all France' (Godechot, 1971, p. 43).

These ideas had their proponents within the Estates-General and the first revolutionary assemblies: indeed, among the most persuasive of monarchists were early political leaders like Cazalès and Maury, men of a deeply conservative character who looked to the King to provide the stability which France required. Yet in the early months of the Revolution their opposition was fragmented and ineffective; despite their numbers – throughout the period from 1789 to 1791 they could muster around three hundred supporters in the chamber – they proved incapable of formulating any agreed alternative programme. This was especially true in 1789 itself, when they could not agree to any counter-measures to resolve the crisis which faced the French people. The more conservative of them rallied to the King's own reform programme, outlined in his *séance royale* of 23 June; and they were outraged by the actions of the Paris crowd in October when Versailles was invaded and the royal family brought back to the capital. But their opposition remained rather inept, perhaps because they were not all motivated by the same desires. Some were absolutists who wanted unreserved powers restored to the Bourbons; others were much more concerned to establish the social position of the nobility or the powers of the clergy, looking to Louis as little more than the means by which those objectives could be achieved; and among the conservatives were many who did not reject the entire revolution, who were thankful that absolutism had been overthrown, and who looked to establish a strong constitutional monarchy in France which could defend their values. They did not form a single party or a coherent interest. Even their social aims were confused. Indeed, the anti-revolutionary language in the early years was bedevilled with contradictions: on the one hand it sought to defend property values against popular violence from the streets; on the other it wanted to capitalize on popular discontent by denouncing the egotism of the bourgeoisie. If opponents of the Revolution emphasized their attachment to Louis, it was partly because the need for monarchy – of whatever kind – was one of the few things that could unite them against the more republican and libertarian elements in revolutionary thinking.

Opposition was not, of course, confined to royalists and aristocrats, nor, indeed, was it all ideologically inspired. In 1789 most men of progressive ideas had been able to rally round general measures like the Declaration of the Rights of Man; but as the Revolution progressed it would define the path of political correctness with ever greater precision, and in the process it created new enemies from within its own ranks. Republicans had little time for constitutional monarchists, nor Jacobins for Girondins. As governments changed with increasing rapidity, it was difficult to keep step, and those who had identified with the previous regime found themselves excluded from influence and denounced as enemies of the Revolution, the republic, the people. By 1793 it would not just be royalists and *émigrés* who were regarded as criminals; in turn that status would be accorded to Feuillants and moderates, Girondins and Dantonists, federalists and Hébertists. After Thermidor those who had been associates of Robespierre were in their turn excluded from the body politic and executed. Political virtue, it was clear, was not divisible. It belonged not to revolutionaries or even republicans, but to the right sort of republicans, those whose ideology coincided with that of the leadership of the day. This had, of course, important consequences for the Revolution itself. It drove many into opposition who had at one time or another been well disposed to the new political order. And it created a pool of alarm and discontent in the country on which those viscerally opposed to the Revolution might hope to draw.

The majority of Frenchmen had little interest in the niceties of Parisian ideology. They had no desire to be harassed and ordered around by others, whether by central government through its decrees and requisitions or through the meddling of local councils, clubs and *commissaires*. And in the eyes of many the Revolution soon became associated with intrusion of this kind. After a brief dawn of liberal reforms and decentralized power the government seemed more and more concerned to control and police, as it sought to root out opponents and guarantee the enactment of the law. The existence of counter-revolution was itself in large part responsible for this tighter, more repressive approach to administration, but that was not how it was perceived in the popular mind. Instead, it was the government which was most often blamed for tiresome controls and restrictions, imposed on the people by a battery of laws and decrees, troops and gendarmes, courts and tribunals. As this perception spread it served to alienate many who had welcomed the liberation which 1789 had brought but who were now increasingly prone to blame their ills on Paris. This was not the achievement of any single party or regime, though the increases in taxation and requisitions after 1793 significantly worsened relations with the centre. Whether under the Jacobin Republic or the Thermidorians, the Directors or the Emperor, the state was increasingly identified with figures of authority – *commissaires* and *agents nationaux*, deputies on mission and prefects, justices of the peace and recruiting sergeants. That authority spread into the smallest local communities as mayors were made increasingly answerable to the Minister of the Interior rather than to the people who had elected them. For many Frenchmen, especially in the villages and hamlets of the countryside, this was an unwelcome intrusion which ran rough-shod over their most precious community traditions. They resented the involvement of outsiders, of townspeople, of bourgeois, in their local affairs. A revolution that had been proclaimed in the name of liberty came increasingly to be seen as dirigiste and oppressive (Montpellier, 1988, pp. 265–96).

This widespread perception did much to destroy such early consensus as existed in favour of the Revolution. For it quickly became apparent that the changes proposed by the revolution-aries could not satisfy everyone, that there were conflicting interests in French society that would not be appeased by appeals to national unity or by the language of fraternity. Insofar as the Revolution restricted itself to dismantling the apparatus of royal government there was a large measure of acceptance among the population at large, since few objected to greater freedoms, to the removal of fiscal burdens or judicial impositions. But the revolutionaries' agenda was always wider than that: in particular, the attack on privilege implied the rejection of some of the most fundamental principles of the eighteenth-century political and social order. And once the Assembly turned to the task of outlining and ultimately imposing its own order, conflict was impossible to avoid. The extent of such conflict, of course, varied. Much of it was relatively muted – the demand for greater regional liberties, for example, or the protests over the administrative division of the country, or the early feminist claims for political rights for women. These were protests limited to particular regions or specific groups, and in the main they could be contained within the new order. But there were other conflicts, created quite specifically by revolutionary policies, which were incapable of resolution. By 1793 large sections of the French population were moved to reject specific revolutionary policies, and with them to challenge the new political and social order which the revolutionaries proposed. The mask of unanimity had dropped.

Those who resisted revolutionary measures were not always ideological counter-revolutionaries. Indeed, the term 'counter-revolution' is deceptive, a part of the persistent and strident propaganda campaign which those in power conducted against their opponents. This was especially so after 1793, when first the Girondins and then the Montagne became highly partisan in their attitude to their opponents, using the rhetoric of counter-revolution to stigmatize those who failed to praise them or to identify with their policies. The Jacobins were, of course, the foremost exponents of this form of denigration, giving their brand of republicanism a monopoly of virtue and castigating all who dared question it as 'moderates', 'counter-revolutionaries', or 'federalists'. But such overtly partisan language did not stop after the ninth of *thermidor*. The Thermidorians and the Directory had every interest in playing their own republican, anti-clerical card, and the same polemical discourse would continue in use until the end of the decade. We should treat it with some caution lest we, too, confuse propaganda for historical fact. Not all those who challenged government policy were opponents of republicanism. In 1794, for instance, many who saw themselves as the defenders of constitutional liberties and representative government might be outraged by Robespierre's terrorist legislation. Opposition was not necessarily linked to royalism, just as rural dissent can be more accurately categorized as a form of popular anti-revolution rather than as part of a counter-revolutionary movement. In the south east, indeed, Colin Lucas suggests that peasant resistance should be recognized for what it was, 'an authentic and radical popular movement just like popular support for the radical revolutionaries' (Nicolas, 1985, p. 484).

Opposition in the provinces

In the new atmosphere which the Revolution created – an atmosphere of hope, in which men might expect that their grievances would be listened to and their views acted upon – society was more volatile, more liable to vent its feelings in explosions of violence. In this sense the King's calling of the Estates-General and his consultation of the population through the *cahiers de doléances* was of fundamental importance. For ordinary people it was the moment when it seemed that their grievances would be answered and they would be freed from the worst abuses of the *ancien régime*. When their aspirations remained unfulfilled, violence could easily ensue. The *Grande Peur* of the summer of 1789 was, as we have seen, the first instance of such violence, but it would not be the last. Between 1789 and 1792 there were several waves of peasant rioting in the French provinces, principally in the traditional *pays de petite culture* of the centre and south of the country. These were not triggered by fear or rumour, but rather by peasant anger –

anger directed at the seigneurs, of course, but also at other targets. For the peasantry was not a single undifferentiated social group or class. Some owned the land they farmed, others were tenants; some were self-sufficient, others depended on the market to make ends meet; in different regions and with different crops security and systems of land tenure varied greatly. In the south west Jean Boutier has shown how, among sharecroppers, it was the rural bourgeoisie and richer peasants to whom rent was due, who were the likeliest target for attack (Boutier, 1979, pp. 760–86). In Gascony, where tithes were high, the Church was widely detested. Anti-urban feeling was often strong, especially where the richer citizens of nearby towns were using their wealth to buy up village land over the heads of the villagers and their sons. When peasant ambitions remained unrealized, when peasants discovered that they were still expected to pay feudal exactions which they thought had been abolished, or when the state's tax burden began to offset the benefits they had obtained, then their anger could turn against the agents of the state itself. Peasant protest, like the peasantry itself, was diffuse and multi-faceted.

If rural opposition had such different causes, so it took very different forms. In some areas peasant revolts continued to be staged through 1791 and 1792 to secure the abolition of the last remnants of feudalism; others remained unmoved and in some, also, radical peasant leaders demanded the implementation of *partage* and the distribution of common lands among the local peasant proprietors; yet elsewhere the issue aroused little enthusiasm and was seen as unworkable. Disputes commonly arose within the rural community between those who had gained and those who had lost from the Revolution – like the bitter antagonisms between proprietors and tenants in Brittany which presaged the outbreak of *chouannerie* (Sutherland, 1982, p. 308). Here again long-standing disputes over land tenures and payments could easily be cloaked in political language and assume a falsely ideological guise (Le Goff, 1981, p. 363). And the traditional distrust of towns, which was a feature of many rural areas, was only heightened by the revolutionary

government. It was not just the rivalry between peasant producers and urban consumers which pitted the peasantry against
their urban neighbours. It was also the huge purchases of *biens
nationaux* made by adroit urban speculators in the rural hinterland which nurtured rural animosity, and the fact that government was so closely concentrated on the towns. During the
Jacobin Republic, for example, it was the towns which supplied
the clubs with their militants; it was the towns which carried
out surveillance and imposed requisitions; it was the towns
from which units ofthe *armée révolutionnaire* set forth to bully
and coerce their rural neighbours. During the Directory little
was done to decentralize authority from the urban centres, until
under Napoleon the whole administrative system revolved
around the *préfecture* in the main town of the department.
Administrative demands and bureaucratic intrusion seemed
quintessentially urban.

Opposition in the capital

The cities, and especially Paris, suffered from popular disorder
of another kind, the disorder of angry crowds and political
demonstrations. There was little new in this: like some of the
traditional areas of peasant *jacquerie* which rediscovered their
former militancy under the guise of revolution, Paris had a long
history of bread riots and political unrest. Its population was a
rich mixture of native Parisians and immigrant workers, the
immigrants generally piled into city-centre lodging houses or
were expelled to the burgeoning popular suburbs. Its markets
were rife with rumour, its wine shops a prey to political
agitation. And the simple fact of being the capital city of France
gave the Parisian crowd an immediacy of impact which its
counterparts in provincial cities could not hope to match. In
Paris, unlike Lyon or Bordeaux, the crowd could bring pressure
on ministers, and this had led governments throughout the
eighteenth century to treat the city with a particular sort of
respect and apprehension. Crowds had regularly formed to

pursue their collective interests or protest some perceived injustice. Public executions, market shortages, and political crises might all lead to violent protest from Paris, a fact which the government had acknowledged in setting up the most efficient urban policing system in Europe. With the spread of political excitement in 1789 it was to be expected that Paris would not stand idly aside, that the popular classes of the capital would involve themselves in the new political process.

Between 1789 and 1795 the Parisian populace would be a constant source of pressure on central government. Political agitators and polemicists fanned out from the Palais Royal to take the message of the Revolution into the popular quarters of the city; newspapers and pamphlets put across to the people a radical revolutionary creed. And though the crowd was always a source of outside pressure on the workings of government – it was never institutionalized into a part of the system – the Parisian *menu peuple* saw themselves as an essential motor of radicalization. They could point to the importance of their role during the summer of 1789, when the taking of the Bastille helped secure the National Assembly and avert the risk of reaction. During that summer disorder in Paris was largely spontaneous, whipped up by orators and popular journalists: similarly the march to Versailles in October 1789 was orchestrated by the women of the Paris markets, angered by the soaring price of bread. But by 1792 Parisian radicals had their own power base in the city's sections and popular societies, with a central mouthpiece in the Commune. They organized popular *journées* in the streets, supporting the Jacobins against their Girondin opponents and demanding greater influence over government decisions. In the more radical of the sectional assemblies the *sans-culottes* urged the introduction of a controlled economy and preached popular sovereignty; they listened to their own egalitarian leaders like Jacques Roux; they read radical newspapers like Marat's *Ami du Peuple* and Hébert's *Père Duchesne*; and they were increasingly fervent in their demand for political surveillance and the use of terror. By the summer of 1794 they could no longer be seen as the simple allies of the Jacobins. Rather they were a distinct opposition movement in their own right, pressing for their own patriotic, puritanical and egalitarian brand of revolutionary politics.

Urban disorder in Paris was contained by a policy of compromise, at least until the overthrow of the Jacobin Republic. The Parisian radicals were allowed to control the streets; they gained important concessions in such matters as price controls and economic terror; under the Jacobins the Commune was given a role in government. In the sections' revolutionary committees they played a part in surveillance and denunciation; through the *armées révolutionnaires* they provided an element of policing. Hanriot, Ronsin and other radical extremists were flattered by a degree of political respectability. Of course the Jacobins' opponents railed against the cynicism of such a popular alliance, denouncing the popular movement as unruly extremists who wanted to reduce the country to a state of anarchy. And once the Jacobins fell no other government was prepared to allow the Paris sections a significant role in decision making. But even in 1794 the sections were held in considerable distrust, as a source of disorder and disunity that was weakening central government. Their ideas of economic equality and popular sovereignty undermined government policy. Their refusal to accept the logic of the free market, their preference for collective bargaining, and their reluctance to abandon their corporate structures all served to provide them with a philosophy that was at variance with that of the government, and hence of the Revolution. Besides, their propaganda in the provinces and in the armies was seen as an attack on Jacobin ideology, and they were denounced as '*hébertistes*' and '*exagérés*'. By the summer of 1794 the full force of the Terror had been turned against the leaders of the sectional movement, which emerged weakened and emasculated. In the Year III two desperate popular *journées*, in *germinal* and *prairial*, marked the last bid by the sections to impose their will on national government. Their risings were ruthlessly swept aside; government had little use – or tolerance – for further disorders in the capital.

Popular unrest outside the capital seldom had the ideological purpose of the Paris sections or enjoyed their structural coherence. In country areas it more commonly took the form of a spontaneous reaction to government policies or government officials, a reaction that might be sparked off by the excessive enthusiasm of local mayors and *commissaires*. Local people were driven to rebel against what they saw as intolerable interference with their time-honoured lifestyle. Their action was a reassertion of the traditional rights of their own community, a rejection of officialdom and of the state's pretensions. In such matters as the ordering of fairs and the regulation of grazing rights local communities had always managed their own affairs, and many were loath to accept regulation from outside. Policing and surveillance caused especial resentment where local people had traditionally enjoyed a degree of autarchy. In two areas, in particular, that resentment was liable to boil over into revolt: in matters of religion and of military recruitment.

Opposition in the Church

The Revolution's policy towards the Catholic Church was a major cause of disaffection, especially among women, who were traditionally more God-fearing than their husbands. Even in 1789 and 1790 the state had been driven to antagonize the Church over such questions as feudal dues, tithes and the Papal states of Avignon and the Comtat Venaissin. In the eyes of the Vatican the Revolution was suspect from the start, with its proclaimed distrust of privilege and its adherence to Enlightened ideals. Anti-clericalism was widespread even during the constitutional monarchy, when the revolutionaries attacked the institution of the Church by abolishing the tithe and nationalizing clerical property. They further antagonized Rome by removing the special Statute of Catholicism and by placing Catholics on an equal footing with other religions. And they attacked religious faith itself by forcing the clergy to take an oath of loyalty to the state, by exiling and executing non-juring

priests, and finally – with the Jacobin campaign of dechristianization – by closing churches and forbidding religious worship.
And although total dechristianization was short-lived, to be
followed by the rather farcical attempt to impose the worship
of the Supreme Being, anti-clericalism did not end with
Robespierre's overthrow. Throughout the Directory the government continued to discourage Catholic practice wherever it
could. Priests who returned from emigration often faced official
persecution, and there were harrowing scenes in Breton villages
when the villagers tried to coerce government *commissaires* into
authorizing the reopening of their churches. Women, as Olwen
Hufton has shown, played an especially notable role in securing
the resumption of Catholic worship (Lewis and Lucas, 1983,
pp. 23–6). Only under Napoleon would any serious attempt be
made to heal the rift between the French state and the religion
of the majority of Frenchmen. Even then the act of healing
would not be complete, with the Petite Eglise holding out
grimly until the restoration of the Bourbons in 1814.

Any attack on religious faith was bound to create bitter
opposition within French society. Deeply held beliefs would
not be discarded to suit political convenience, and in Catholic
areas of the country non-juring priests could be assured of wide
popular support. But beliefs varied hugely from region to
region: France as a whole was no longer a devoutly Catholic
country by the last years of the *ancien régime*. There were areas
where religious faith ran deep, areas like the west and Brittany,
the southern Massif Central and parts of the south east,
Flanders and the Pays Basque. Here priest and parishioner
stood side by side against the advance of rationalism and
godlessness: priests could refuse the civic oath with relative
confidence, knowing that their flock would support them,
protect them, and if necessary rebel for them against the
Revolutionary state. The Jacobins may have been exaggerating
when they saw the hand of refractory clergy behind every
rumbling of rural disaffection, but the notion was not of itself
absurd. For in regions such as the west the religious issue
would leave deep social and political scars, to the extent that it

dominated the political agenda. Opposition to the Revolution in Brittany, for instance, was fuelled by the Revolution's religious intolerance and by its effect on a deeply Catholic population. Elsewhere – for example, in large areas of Provence and Aquitaine – the extent of religious practice was already much diminished by the middle of the eighteenth century, and here anti-clericalism enjoyed considerable popular support. Deputies on mission would be cheered when they ordered the closure of churches, local clubs would urge new measures against the clergy, and the new secular ceremonies would be eagerly adopted. Already in the late eighteenth century there were two Frances in religious terms; what the Revolution did was to drive a powerful wedge between them, ensuring that the clerical–anticlerical schism remained an important determinant of political loyalty throughout much of the nineteenth and twentieth centuries (Vovelle, 1991, pp. 151–3).

Quite apart from ideological considerations the Revolution's attack on the Church had an important cultural dimension which helps explain the intensity of popular reaction. For what was under attack, in the eyes of local people, was often not the distant hierarchy of the Catholic establishment, but the Catholic presence in their village. In particular, it was the village church that was threatened, and the village church occupied a position in the life of many rural communities that transcended the Roman communion. The church was the centre of the parish, where village meetings were generally held; it was often the sole fount of education and poor relief; and in times of distress and calamity the church bells would be rung to summon the men back from the fields. Hence the attack on religion was an assault on more than Catholic consciences; it was also an assault on village traditions and village liberties, with which Catholic practice and Catholic ritual were deeply intertwined. For much of eighteenth century popular religion was little different from traditional superstition: that is what, for many peasant communities, gave it its strength. People prayed to their saints for a good harvest or got the priest to bless sick cows and sheep. Religious festivals faithfully reflected the ebb and flow of the agricultural year. And it was these age-old traditions and practices which the Revolution sought to undermine: by 1795, it had, in the words of Suzanne Desan, 'created a whole cultural system of revolutionary rituals, symbols and language which aimed to replace Christianity' and sought to re-educate people according to its own ideals and values (Desan, 1990, p. 2). Of course there was resistance. When the young men of a village rallied to protect their priest from arrest, they were not just defending the Catholic Church against Anti-Christ. More importantly, perhaps, they were performing their time-honoured function as the defenders of the community against outside threats.

Other reasons for discontent

The other major catalyst to unrest was military service, which became a source of popular discontent as the scale of warfare grew and the government's demands became increasingly relentless. It was widely accepted that new recruitment techniques were necessary, and that the methods used for the old royal army were insufficient to the needs of revolutionary warfare. France could no longer depend on press gangs and on regiments of foreign mercenaries; and the crisis of the early 1790s, with officers tendering their resignations and deserting in droves, often taking their men with them, and with soldiers mutinying or joining the National Guard, made reform an urgent necessity (Scott, 1978, pp. 81–108). Besides, the ideals of the Revolution seemed incompatible with the regiments that were inherited from the *ancien régime*: the armies, after all, were supposed to take the libertarian message of 1789 to the peoples of Europe. The practical problems were enormous. How could the huge numbers needed to fight a long war against the massed powers of Europe be found and trained? And how could the methods of recruitment be so changed as to provide a new kind of army, one that would be consistent with the Revolution's own ideals? There would be no easy answer. After attempting to meet the needs of the armies by voluntarism alone, the Revolutionaries were forced to enforce local quotas, until in 1799 these gave way to regular annual conscriptions. In other words, they turned to various forms of compulsion, at least in those areas of the country which failed to provide their battalions of genuine volunteers. But compulsion was bitterly resisted and balloting denounced as a new version of the hated militia service of the eighteenth century. This was particularly so in country areas lacking any established tradition of soldiering. There resistance and evasion would remain a constant thorn in the government's side.

Resistance was not, of course, universal: there were regions of the country which patriotically produced their quotas of soldiers for the national cause. But in large areas of the south and west, in particular, it was endemic, and it proved almost impossible to root out. Such resistance took a number of time-honoured forms, its scale magnified by the scale of the wars and by the sheer size of the government's demands. Some feigned ill-health or mutilated themselves to avoid the draft; others turned to precipitate or fraudulent marriages; those who could afford to bought a substitute. But the most common forms of draft-evasion, and those which most seriously worried the government, were *insoumission* and desertion, which were still posing serious problems for Napoleon in 1809 and 1810. Nor was the deserter an isolated individual, alienated from the rest of society. The alarming aspect of the problem for the government was the fact that he could generally be assured of support from within his community or the community where he was in hiding – from his parents and neighbours, from farmers anxious to find cheap labour, from mayors who took pity on him, from his peer group, the young village boys who identified easily with his plight. In large areas of the country the patriotic appeal of the Revolution counted for little: during the Revolution and Empire several hundred thousand young Frenchmen would choose the route of desertion or draft evasion rather than submit to the discipline of the regiments. And when the government tried to intervene, when gendarmes came in to the village or garrisons were imposed on the villagers, their sullen resentment was clear to all. Gendarmes were stoned and threatened; on odd occasions they were killed. When the young men risked arrest the response could even be a full-blown riot. With stronger policing and the use of troops against recalcitrant villages – the hated *colonnes mobiles* that were deployed under the Directory – the government might hope to make the option of resistance less attractive. But the problem was never eliminated. And Paris paid a heavy price in hatred and resentment (Forrest, 1989, pp. 219–37).

Religion, military service, and the defence of local culture were all elements which helped explain the outbreaks of counter-revolution during the 1790s. In Brittany *chouannerie* bred on social discontents, especially the discontents of tenant-farmers; but it also had an important religious dimension, with Catholic Breton villages alienated from the Revolution and refractory priests who offered shelter and support. Farther south, the six departments of the west that constitute the *Vendée militaire* rose in rebellion in response to the recruitment demands of March 1793. But again the root causes of the rebellion ran deeper, and the support enjoyed by the young in their village communities must be explained in social terms. As Paul Bois and Charles Tilly have shown, tensions between town and country played a major part in fomenting rebellion in a region where the Revolution was closely identified with the towns and their political clubs. The insensitive demands of urban Patriots and Jacobins helped rally countrymen to the standard of revolt – their open contempt for rural culture, their raucous support for the *armées révolutionnaires*, their premature and exaggerated commitment to dechristianization. For local revolutionaries could be utterly insensitive in their dealings with the countryside, showing scant respect for the fears and traditions of others. In the south east, for instance, Catholic counter-revolution was encouraged by the anti-clericalism of the Protestant urban elite who ran the early Revolution in the Gard. And in the Vaucluse – the former Comtat Venaissin – the conflict between the Catholic hinterland and the Republican city of Avignon was greatly embittered by the excesses of the Avignonnais Patriot leader, the aptly named Jourdan Coupe-têtes.

The form and language of revolt varied from place to place, with some of the outbreaks more openly royalist than others. The link between opposition and rural catholicism, however, was often strong. At the camp de Jalès in the Gard Catholic royalists assembled in 1791 with the specific aim of attacking the supporters of the Revolution in nearby towns like Uzès; here the royalists looked for support in Catholic villages while the municipal authorities appealed for reinforcements from the Protestant villages of the Gardon valley (Lewis, 1978, p. 32). In the west and in parts of the south refractory priests, returning from exile in Spain, took an active part in fomenting discontent against a republic they denounced as Anti-Christ. In the west, again, local nobles often offered their support, and peasants would once again find themselves fighting under the traditional noble leadership of their communities. Some, like Puisaye and d'Antraïgues, plotted the overthrow of the government, corresponding with the Bourbons in exile or making use of secret networks of spies and supporters. So, too, the Allier brothers, among the most powerful of the clerico-royalist leaders in the south, convinced the *émigré* court in Koblenz that there would soon be a massive counter-revolutionary movement throughout the Midi that would sweep the revolutionaries from power. In Brittany Puisaye worked closely with English agents, and funds supplied by the English secret service helped to lubricate the wheels of revolt: by 1797 the English government was even prepared to work with the insurgents in a disastrous military operation on the Quiberon peninsula (Hutt, 1983, pp. 272–323). Jacobin suspicions about English gold were not without foundation. But notions of a consolidated plot were wildly exaggerated. Opponents of the Revolution argued endlessly among themselves about both the political and the social order they wished to impose. Indeed, not all rural counter-revolutionaries embraced the idea of monarchy, and those who did were often bitterly divided about what sort of monarchy they wanted. There was no single or coherent counter-revolutionary cause.

What all would seem to have shared was a sense that they were defending their own values and their own people against attack from outsiders, from people intent on destroying their local traditions. It was by appealing to this sense of localism that they recruited young men for the rebel armies, among them many who had already deserted from the armies of the Republic. For in the areas of rural counter-revolution the Republic's nationalist ideology had little impact: it was the insensitive centralism of the Revolution, impervious, it seemed, to local needs and local culture, which was deeply resented. In the name of national unity, of 'the one and indivisible nation', the government made few concessions to history or to tradition. Under the Jacobins, indeed, the Convention went out of its way to suppress cultural diversity, imposing French as the 'language of liberty' and condemning the use of local dialects and regional languages. As Bertrand Barère argued in a tellingly perverse passage, these were the languages of unrest and insurrection. 'Federalism and superstition speak Bas-Breton; emigration and hatred of the Republic speak German; counter-revolution speaks Italian, and fanaticism speaks Basque. Let us break these harmful instruments of error' (De Certeau et al., 1975, p. 295).

In such circumstances it is hardly surprising that the Parisian revolution was so widely rejected in the more peripheral regions of France. This rejection was not necessarily associated with a royalist ideology or with a desire to restore the social hierarchies of the *ancien régime*. Insurrection did not have to be counter-revolutionary. In many parts of the countryside it was little more than a plea to be left alone, spared the successive intrusions of the outside world. There was even a sense in which the insurgents were rebelling in the cause of order, of their traditional autarchy and custom. For in the eyes of many provincial Frenchmen it was the Republic which posed the real threat to established order – disrupting religion, destroying clerical education, and undermining long-standing traditions. It was the Republic which, by calling the young men away from the fields to serve on the frontier, broke up families and created a severe shortage of labour for agriculture. It was the Republic, too, which forbade their traditional festivals and village festivities and denied them their freedom on Sundays (the *décadi*, one day off in ten, was a poor substitute). By 1794, moreover, the image of the Republic in many parts of the country had become that of an unwelcome predator, sacrificing everything and everyone to the needs of war. Its *commissaires* stole their corn and requisitioned their horses. Its soldiers brought violence and bloodshed. In the west, especially, the Republic would forever be associated with Turreau's *colonnes infernales*, burning villages, looting grain, and slaughtering all who stood in their path. It was an image not of order but of anarchy.

Fear of anarchy also helps explain the urban opposition during the summer of 1793, when many of the most important provincial cities – among them Lyon, Marseille and Bordeaux – declared that they no longer recognized the authority of the Convention (Edmonds, 1990; Scott, 1973; Forrest, 1975). They denounced the Jacobin seizure of power and alleged that the Convention was no longer free, since twenty-nine of its members had been arbitrarily arrested. Resuming their own share of sovereignty they set up executive commissions, sought support from neighbouring departments and, in some cases, raised local armies with the express aim of sending troops against Paris. The Jacobins denounced such insurrections as 'federalist' and tried to associate them in the public mind with the Vendée and rural counter-revolution. But in reality the two forms of opposition had little in common. The federalist cities were neither royalist nor Catholic. Their leaders were often lawyers and merchants of considerable substance and political experience; and they enjoyed the support of a popular movement in the form of the sectional assemblies. If federalism implied a desire to set up a system of federal republics and to destroy national unity, they were not federalist either. So why did they revolt? They were to some degree acting out of desperation, a desire to protect themselves and their battered economies from further damage. As Paul Hanson has argued in his discussion of the contrasting politics of Caen and Limoges, 'the social fabric and economic structures of a town and region are crucial factors in moulding the shape of the local political arena' (Hanson, 1989, p. 246). But their fears were more commonly political than economic. Often the principal targets of their anger were local club militants who preached terror and who had in some cases already seized power locally. They were, they claimed, committed republicans, loyal to the ideals of the Revolution and to the constitutional liberties which were now being so blatantly neglected. The Jacobins, of course, countered that they were a privileged and plutocratic elite, intent on holding on to power at the expense of others; by doing so they avoided answering the federalists' political case. And Jacobin propaganda was greatly helped when in August of 1793 the naval port of Toulon joined Marseille in revolt, handing over its arsenal, naval installations and a number of warships to the British (Crook, 1991, pp. 126–57). Federalism could then be shown to be treacherous as well as counter-revolutionary (Edmonds, 1983, p. 26).

The anti-Jacobin movement in the cities – a much more accurate description than federalist – was in no sense counter-revolutionary. It did not seek to challenge the legitimacy of republican institutions. Real counter-revolution was a rural phenomenon, and the areas where counter-revolution was rampant were, almost by definition, areas where the writ of national government barely ran. Such areas, often close to frontiers or protected by natural physical barriers like mountain ranges, were difficult to police, especially where traditions of crime and banditry were deeply rooted. Indeed, the distinction between the activities of counter-revolutionary bands and bands of common criminals was often dangerously blurred. Both lived in semi-clandestinity, ready to take refuge should the gendarmes approach; neither showed any compunction about acts of robbery and murder; their integration into the local community would seem to have been equally strong. The only tangible distinction might lie in their choice of victim and in the justification which they used for their crimes. The royalist terror gangs of the south east, for instance, robbed republican mail coaches and stole republican gold. They stole for Christ and King. In the White Terror of 1795 and 1796 they also murdered freely for Christ and King, selecting as their targets those in the community who were known for their republican sympathies, who had served on revolutionary committees or tribunals, or whose evidence had helped condemn royalists and aristocrats. There was little that the Revolution could do to stop such excesses, since the police were incapable of making arrests and cowed juries refused to convict. By the end of the Directory there were still areas of the south where no republican could travel in safety and where brigandage went unchecked. Increasingly, the White Terror merged into simple brigandage, with killing and robbing their own reward. The feared brigand leaders of the south east, like Saint-Christol and Dominique Allier, were bandits before they were royalists. Their opposition to the Revolution had become almost incidental (Lewis and Lucas, 1983, pp. 195–231).

It was only during the Napoleonic period that the government succeeded in rooting out this basic lawlessness from French society. How was this achieved? In part it can be ascribed to economic policies which allocated high prices to farm produce and won support for the regime from the majority of peasants. For that in turn led to the brigands being disowned by the communities which had sheltered them. In part, too, Napoleon benefited from the desire of the French people for stability: the population was tired of turmoil and political upheaval and was eager to accept an imposed order if it would guarantee social peace. But the defeat of banditry owed more to policing and powers of repression than to public opinion. It was a mission which Napoleon pursued with determination and ruthless efficiency, aware that the stability of his entire regime depended on his success in imposing the rule of law. His achievement in this regard is impressive, though we must not forget that he had a far more sophisticated structure of administration and police than any available to the Revolution. Through the prefects he gathered information on the activities of the bands and on those who offered them protection. The gendarmerie was given the specific task of breaking up the last of the brigand gangs, supported where necessary by units of the army. And if juries would not convict, special courts would, courts composed of benches of judges with unequivocal instructions to destroy the gangs and execute their leaders. By 1804 the last of the great terror gangs had been broken and the disorder that had been endemic throughout much of the countryside was effectively brought to an end.

The Revolution: an evaluation

Throughout the Revolution resistance had posed a constant problem for the authorities, and, despite its discourse of unity, Paris had never succeeded in quelling the opposition of large parts of the population. This opposition was not restricted to privileged elites or to cliques of royalists and aristocrats. In many areas it was a popular movement in its own right, as popular, perhaps, as the radicalism of the Paris sections. For the revolutionaries could hardly avoid making enemies. They attempted to change the very foundations of French society and the ways in which Frenchmen related to one another; they abolished corporate structures; they tried to mould an individualistic society where previously there had been legal estates and privileges. These were colossal changes, demanding another revolution, a revolution in popular mentalities and perceptions. They were, moreover, changes which risked mobilizing people at opposite ends of the political spectrum – peasants fearful of losing their lands to the bourgeois of nearby towns, communities united in defence of their traditional religion, and Parisian artisans whose radical political ideas were not matched by a belief in economic individualism. Where existing interests suffered, opposition was only to be expected, and that opposition, as we have seen, often turned into political and even military resistance.

The danger was more acute in that the government lacked

the means to police its reforms effectively, while there were whole areas of the country where opposition was widespread. It is in this sense that counter-revolution should be seen as an integral part of the revolutionary experience. It acted as a powerful catalyst to centralization and repression. Indeed, if foreign war was responsible for many of the new demands which the revolutionaries made of the civilian population, then counter-revolution had an equally important effect on national policy. The existence within France of sizeable groups opposed to the revolutionary programme forced Paris to crystallize its approach and to abandon constitutionalism in favour of greater control. Citizenship became more carefully defined, its benefits more selectively bestowed. The Revolution became less a revolution of all the French people than a revolution of those who were dependable, those who supported its policies, those who were virtuous. It is in this sense, as Donald Sutherland has demonstrated, that the counter-revolution changed the priorities and the direction of revolutionary France, to the extent that 'the whole history of the period can be understood as the struggle against a counter-revolution that was not so much aristocratic as massive, extensive, durable and popular' (Sutherland, 1985, p. 14).

Guide to Further Reading

The French Revolution has generated such a plethora of discussion and controversy that no short bibliographical guide can do more than suggest further avenues for exploration. Of general books on the period D. M. G. Sutherland's *France, 1789–1815: Revolution and counter-revolution* is clearly written and thematically organized, while William Doyle's *Oxford history of the French Revolution* gives an excellent synthesis of current literature and a strongly political interpretation of the Revolution. J. F. Bosher's *The French Revolution* is political in emphasis, though it also contains a useful section on the French economy. For the classic social interpretation, one has to turn to George Lefebvre's two-volume work on *The French Revolution*, or to Albert Soboul's more polemically Marxist analysis in *The French Revolution, 1787–1799*. General works offering a cultural approach include Lynn Hunt, *Politics, culture and class in the French Revolution*; and the collection of articles by Keith Baker, *Interpreting the French Revolution*. This places a strong emphasis on revolutionary discourse, as does François Furet in *Revolutionary France, 1770–1880*. A rather different cultural approach is offered by Emmet Kennedy's *A Cultural History of the French Revolution*, which lays greater emphasis on art and cultural artefacts. Shorter introductions to the period are provided by J. M. Roberts, *The French Revolution*, largely sympathetic to the revisionist stance; and Gwynne Lewis, *The French Revolution: Rethinking the Debate*, which attempts to balance the political, economic and cultural views of the Revolution and gives considerable weight to economic and social issues. Those seeking a useful and accessible reference work on the period should consult Colin Jones, *The Longman companion to the French Revolution*.

The debate on the origins of the Revolution has been vigorous and frequently bitter, and though these technically lie outside the scope of this volume, some bibliographical guidance may be useful. George Lefebvre's *The coming of the French Revolution* presents the classic French treatment of the subject, but his neat division of the revolutionary movement into social categories (aristocratic, bourgeois, peasant and popular) has increasingly come under attack, first by Alfred Cobban in his *Social interpretation of the French Revolution*, then, more robustly, by William Doyle in his *Origins of the French Revolution*. It is clear, indeed, that in recent years a social explanation of the Revolution has become more and more difficult to sustain – a view that is well discussed by T. C. W. Blanning in his concise pamphlet on *The French Revolution: aristocrats versus bourgeois?*. But to say that the causes of the Revolution are largely political begs the wider question of what constituted politics in the *ancien régime*. For John Bosher much can be explained by the failure of the King to control his finances (*French finances, 1770–1795: from business to bureaucracy*). Others, like Norman Hampson, stress the importance of intellectual origins – both in *The Enlightenment* and, more recently, in *Will and circumstance*, where he points to the competing intellectual influences of Montesquieu and Rousseau. Robert Darnton discusses the role of pamphleteers and journalists in *The literary underground of the old regime*, as do a cluster of historians of the eighteenth-century press, including Harvey Chisick, Jack Censer and Jeremy Popkin. The most cogent analysis of domestic politics in the months immediately preceding 1789 remains Jean Egret, *The French Pre-revolution, 1787–89*. But if Bailey Stone is right, historians should be looking beyond the purely domestic sphere. In his recent work of synthesis, *The genesis of the French Revolution*, he argues that the fall of the *ancien régime* had as much to do with failures in foreign policy as with the monarchy's failure to remain in touch with political, social and intellectual movements in France itself.

Many of these works are concerned, of course, with the collapse of the old regime rather than with the origins of the Revolution – and it may be important for us to retain a distinction between the two. There has been a great deal of innovative research on the last twenty or thirty years of the Bourbon monarchy to which students of the Pre-revolution can turn with profit. Among the more interesting approaches are those of Dale Van Kley (*The Damiens Affair and the unravelling of the ancien régime, 1750–1770*) and Sara Maza (*Private lives and public affairs: the causes célèbres of pre-Revolutionary France*), both of whom emphasize the political culture of the eighteenth-century world. The professional culture of the law is the subject of a number of monographs on barristers, *parlementaires* and others; see especially David Bell's *Lawyers and citizens: the making of a political elite in old regime France* and Richard Mowery Andrews' *Law, magistracy and crime in old regime Paris, 1735–89*. The complex culture of the workplace has been dissected, with notably differing conclusions, by both William H. Sewell jnr. (*Work and Revolution in France: the language of labor from the old regime to 1848*) and Michael Sonenscher (*Work and wages: natural law, politics and the eighteenth-century French trades*). Keith Baker, in *Inventing the French Revolution*, offers a stimulating discussion of the language of politics at the end of the *ancien régime*. His edited collection of papers, entitled *The political culture of the old regime*, provides a thoughtful introduction to the complex structures of the period and to the whole notion of a public sphere in eighteenth-century France.

The political history of the Revolution is well covered in most of the general textbooks, especially those by Doyle and Lefebvre. For the period of constitutional monarchy, arguably the least chewed over by historians, note the differing views presented in Norman Hampson's *Prelude to Terror* and in

Michel Vovelle's *The fall of the French monarchy, 1789–92*. In *Citizens* Simon Schama spends an exceptional amount of time on the *ancien régime* and barely gets beyond the constitutional period. Useful accounts of the adjustment required of particular groups to the Revolution can be found in Gail Bossenga, *The politics of privilege*, which concentrates on Lille, and Michael Fitzsimmons's work on *The Parisian order of barristers*. Fitzsimmons has also examined the debates on the 1791 Constitution and the process by which sovereignty was passed from the monarch to the nation (*The Remaking of France: the National Assembly and the Constitution of 1791*). John Hardman's *Louis XVI*, published in 1993 to mark the bicentenary of the King's execution, is the best biography of a monarch who has not been well served by historians. Louis's trial has been dissected in far more detail. See D. P. Jordan, *The king's trial*, and Michael Walzer, *Regicide and Revolution*.

For the republican period, the best introduction remains Michael Sydenham's *The First French Republic*. On the various political groups see Alison Patrick, *The men of the First French Republic*, which attempts to place Girondins and Jacobins in context. On the Gironde there is Sydenham's earlier work, *The Girondins*, as well as Gary Kates's useful and thought-provoking study of *The Cercle Social*. The Jacobins are best served by Michael Kennedy's two volumes, soon to be supplemented by a third, on *The Jacobin clubs*. Among the better biographies available in English are Louis Gottshalk on *Lafayette* and Norman Hampson's two biographies, *Danton* and *The life and times of Maximilien Robespierre*. On the fall of Robespierre see Richard Bienvenu, *The ninth of Thermidor*. For the period after Thermidor, the best political works are still those of Lefebvre on *The Thermidorians* and *The Directory*, though these should be supplemented by Martyn Lyons, *France under the Directory*, and by the volume of essays edited by Colin Lucas and Gwynne Lewis entitled *Beyond the Terror*. See also the various contributors to Lucas (ed.), *The political culture of the French Revolution*.

The most accessible introduction to a study of the Terror is Norman Hampson's pamphlet on *The Terror in the French*

Revolution; a good statistical survey of its impact can be found in Donald Greer's ageing but invaluable *The incidence of the Terror in the French Revolution.* For the members of the Committee of Public Safety see R. R. Palmer, *Twelve who ruled,* an interesting exercise in collective biography. On the meaning and symbolism of Terror, Lynn Hunt has interesting things to say, as do Mona Ozouf in her *Festivals of the French Revolution* and François Furet in *Interpreting the French Revolution.* A good and recent collection of thematic essays is Keith Baker (ed.), *The Terror,* the fourth volume in the Bicentenary series on 'The French Revolution and the Creation of Modern Political Culture'. But the Terror can only really be understood on the ground, as it was enacted at local level, a subject best tackled in Colin Lucas's monograph, *The structure of the Terror,* on Javogues and the Department of the Loire.

On the important contribution of the Paris popular movement to the politics of Terror, see Soboul, *The Parisian sans-culottes and the French Revolution*; Gwyn Williams, *Artisans and sans-culottes*; and R. B. Rose, *The making of the sans-culottes.* To understand the complex mentality of the people of Paris it may be necessary to study their evolution over a longer timespan. Among the best recent works on eighteenth-century Paris are Daniel Roche, *The people of Paris*; Arlette Farge, *Fragile lives: violence, power and solidarity in eighteenth-century Paris*; David Garrioch, *Neighbourhood and community in Paris, 1740–90.* The contribution of women is noted by D. G. Levy, H. B. Applewhite and M. D. Johnson in their edited collection of sources, *Women in revolutionary Paris, 1789–95.* Also invaluable are Richard Cobb's work on *The people's armies* as agents of terror and his more general discussion in *The police and the people.*

For the religious history of the Revolution the most accessible introduction is J. McManners, *The French Revolution and the Church*; or start with chapter 2 of R. Gibson, *A social history of French Catholicism.* Timothy Tackett has produced two more detailed studies of the Church in this period: *Priest and parish in eighteenth-century France,* which discusses the role played by the Church in the community, and *Religion, revolu-*

tion and regional culture in eighteenth-century France: the eccle-siastical oath of 1791, a detailed study of the Civil Constitution and of responses to it. For the Revolution's policy, and especially for a discussion of dechristianization, see Michel Vovelle, *The revolution against the Church*, while popular religion is broached by Suzanne Desan, *Reclaiming the sacred: lay religion and popular politics in revolutionary France*. See also Frank Tallett's chapter 'Dechristianising France', in F. Tallett and N. Atkin (eds), *Religion, society and politics in France since 1789*.

Revolutionary propaganda was also strongly anti-clerical. On art, good recent studies include Emmet Kennedy, *A cultural history of the French Revolution*, James Leith, *The idea of art as propaganda in France*, and Dorothy Johnson, *Jacques-Louis David: art in metamorphosis*. The Paris book trade has its historian in Carla Hesse, *Publishing and cultural politics in revolutionary Paris*. For the press see Hugh Gough's encyclo-paedic study of *The newspaper press in the French Revolution*. Others to broach the subject of Revolutionary newspapers include Jack Censer, *Prelude to power: the Parisian radical press, 1789–91*, and, on the other side, Jeremy Popkin, *The right-wing press in France, 1792–1800*. Popkin has also given us a more general survey, *Revolutionary news: the press in France, 1789–99*.

Peasant interests and peasant politics are discussed by P. M. Jones in his study of *The peasantry in the French Revolution*. For the Grande Peur of 1789 – arguably the most important con-tribution made by the peasantry – the classic work of Georges Lefebvre, *The Great Fear*, remains unsurpassed. A good local study is Clay Ramsay, *The ideology of the Great Fear: the Soissonnais in 1789*. On the impact of the Revolution on the rural economy, the best recent work is in article form. See especially the long chapter by Le Goff and Sutherland in A. Forrest and P. M. Jones (eds), *Reshaping France: town, country and region in the French Revolution*. The economy, indeed, is an area that has been far better treated by French than by English scholars. In English there is not much to turn to besides the relevant parts of G. Lewis, *The French Revolution: rethinking the debate*, and Florin Aftalion, *The French Revolution: an economic interpretation*, which gives a somewhat polemical and monetarist view. For the impact of Revolutionary policies on the poor and poor relief, see Colin Jones, *Charity and bienfaisance*, a study of the city of Montpellier, and Alan Forrest, *The French Revolution and the poor*. In the growing field of medical history one of the best recent works is Dora Weiner, *The citizen–patient in Revolutionary and Imperial Paris*. And for a discussion of the impact of the Revolution on French eductional provision, especially primary education, see Isser Woloch's stimulating synthesis, *The new regime: transformations of the French civic order, 1789–1820s*.

The history of French provincial towns during the Revolution has been relatively thoroughly researched, especially of those towns which became involved in the federalist revolt. The best of them attempt to link federalism with the cities' earlier revolutionary experience. On Lyon, for instance, there is W. D. Edmonds's excellent *Jacobinism and the revolt of Lyon, 1789–93*. Other studies of federalist cities include Paul Hanson's comparative treatment of Caen and Limoges in *Provincial politics in the French Revolution*; William Scott, *Terror and repression in revolutionary Marseilles*; Malcolm Crook, *Toulon in war and Revolution*; and Forrest, *Society and politics in revolutionary Bordeaux*. Note, also, Lynn Hunt's comparative study of Troyes and Reims, *Urban politics in the French Revolution*, and Ted Margadant's path-breaking study of inter-urban disputes, *Urban rivalries in the French Revolution*.

Federalism was, of course, distinct from counter-revolution, a subject to which there is no good general introduction, though Sutherland's textbook on *France, 1789–1815: Revolution and counter-revolution* makes an excellent job of putting it in a wider context. Jacques Godechot's *Counter-revolution: doctrine and action* is comprehensive, if somewhat dated. Peasant insurrection in the west of France is uncovered in Charles Tilly, *The Vendée*; T. J. A. Le Goff, *Vannes and its region*; and D. M. G. Sutherland, *The Chouans*. There is much more in French. Plots, foreign agents and émigré nobles abound; see especially Maurice Hutt's exhaustive study of *Chouannerie and counter-*

revolution: Puisaye, the princes and the British government in the 1790s. For a study of counter-revolution in the south east, see Lewis, *The Second Vendée* on the Department of the Gard. This also covers the White Terror after 1795. In this regard see also David Higg's book on *Ultraroyalism in Toulouse*, and François Gendron's study of the *jeunesse dorée, The gilded youth after thermidor.* More generally, much can be gained from consulting Richard Cobb's *Reactions to the French Revolution*, a series of essays which concentrate on the directorial years. Not all opposition in that period came from the right, however, as Isser Woloch demonstrates in *Jacobin legacy: the Jacobin movement under the Directory.* Among neo-Jacobins none gained greater notoriety than Babeuf; a good biography is Rose, *Gracchus Babeuf, the first revolutionary communist.*

The nature and impact of war have also been extensively analysed. For a discussion of its causes see Blanning, *The origins of the French revolutionary wars*, which pours a certain amount of cold water on ideological interpretations. The problems of the French armies in the early part of the Revolution are discussed in Sam Scott's *The response of the royal army to the French Revolution*, while the armies of the Republic are the subject of Jean-Paul Bertaud's *The army of the French Revolution.* J. A. Lynn's *The bayonets of the Republic* discusses motivation and tactics in France's biggest army, the Armée du Nord. Alan Forrest deals with conscription problems in *Conscripts and deserters: the army and French society during the Revolution and Empire*, and offers a more general conspectus of the period in *The soldiers of the French Revolution.* The lot of army veterans, an increasingly powerful pressure group, is the subject of Isser Woloch's *The French veteran from the Revolution to the Restoration.* And the experience of the French abroad, in the countries which they invaded or where they set up sister republics, has been thoroughly studied. Among the best monographs on the Revolution outside France are Blanning's *The French Revolution in Germany*; Schama's *Patriots and liberators: Revolution in the Netherlands, 1780–1813*; and Marianne Elliott's *Partners in Revolution: the United Irishmen and France.*

Bibliography and References

Ado, Anatoli, 1987: *Les paysans et la Révolution française: le mouve-ment paysan en 1789–1794*. Moscow: Moscow University Press (in Russian).

Aftalion, Florin 1990: *The French Revolution: an economic interpreta-tion*. Cambridge: Cambridge University Press.

Agulhon, Maurice 1981: *Marianne into battle: republican imagery and symbolism in France, 1789–1880*. Cambridge: Cambridge University Press.

Baker, Keith (ed.) 1987: *The political culture of the old regime*. Oxford: Pergamon Press.

Benot, Yves 1988: *La Révolution Française et la fin des colonies*. Paris: La Découverte.

Bergeron, Louis 1981: *France under Napoleon*. Princeton: Princeton University Press.

Berlanstein, Lenard 1975: *The barristers of Toulouse in the eighteenth century, 1740–93*. Baltimore: Johns Hopkins University Press.

Bertaud, Jean-Paul 1989: *The army of the French Revolution: from citizen-soldiers to instruments of power*. Princeton: Princeton Univer-sity Press.

Blanning, T. C. W. 1986: *The origins of the French revolutionary wars*. London: Longman.

Bosher, J. F. 1988: *The French Revolution*. New York: Norton.

Bossenga, Gail 1991: *The politics of privilege: old regime and Revolution in Lille*. Cambridge: Cambridge University Press.

Boutier, Jean 1979: 'Jacqueries en pays croquant: les révoltes paysannes en Aquitaine, décembre 1789–mars 1790'. *Annales: Economies, Sociétés, Civilisations*, 34, 760–86.

Campbell, Peter Robert 1988: *The ancien regime in France*. Oxford: Basil Blackwell.

Censer, Jack 1976: *Prelude to power: the Parisian radical press, 1789–91*. Baltimore: Johns Hopkins University Press.

Chaussinand-Nogaret, Guy 1985: *The French nobility in the eighteenth century: from feudalism to enlightenment*. Cambridge: Cambridge University Press.

Chisick, Harvey 1992: *The production, distribution and readership of a conservative journal of the early French Revolution: the Ami du Roi of the Abbé Royou*. Philadelphia: American Philosophical Society.

Chomel, Vital (ed.) 1988: *Les débuts de la Révolution française en Dauphiné, 1788–91*. Grenoble: Presses Universitaires de Grenoble.

Church, Clive 1981: *Revolution and red tape: the French ministerial bureaucracy, 1770–1850*. Oxford: Clarendon Press.

Cobb, Richard 1969: *A second identity: essays on France and French history*. London: Oxford University Press.

Cobb, Richard 1987: *The people's armies* (tr. Marianne Elliott). London: Yale University Press.

Cobban, Alfred 1964: *The social interpretation of the French Revolution*. Cambridge: Cambridge University Press.

Cole, Alistair and Campbell, Peter 1989: *French electoral systems and elections since 1789*. Aldershot: Gower.

Crook, Malcolm 1991: *Toulon in war and revolution*. Manchester: Manchester University Press.

Darnton, Robert 1982: *The literary underground of the old regime*. Cambridge, Mass.: Harvard University Press.

De Certeau, Michel, Julia, Dominique and Revel, Jacques 1975: *Une politique de la langue: la Révolution française et les patois*. Paris: Gallimard.

Desan, Suzanne 1990: *Reclaiming the sacred: lay religion and popular politics in revolutionary France*. Ithaca: Cornell University Press.

Doyle, William 1980: *Origins of the French Revolution*. Oxford: Oxford University Press.

Doyle, William 1989: *The Oxford history of the French Revolution*. Oxford: Clarendon Press.

Edmonds, W. D. 1983: 'Federalism and urban revolt'. *Journal of Modern History*, 55, 22–53.

Edmonds, W. D. 1990: *Jacobinism and the revolt of Lyon, 1789–93.* Oxford: Clarendon Press.

Ellery, Eloise 1915: *Brissot de Warville: a study in the history of the French Revolution.* Boston: Houghton Mifflin Company.

Emmanuelli, François-Xavier 1977:'De la conscience politique à la naissance du "provincialisme" 'dans la Généralité d'Aix à la fin du dix-huitième siècle'. In C. Gras and G. Livet (eds) *Régions et régionalisme en France du 18e siècle à nos jours*; 117–38.

Fitzsimmons, Michael 1987: *The Parisian order of barristers and the French Revolution.* Cambridge, Mass.: Harvard University Press.

Forrest, Alan 1975: *Society and politics in revolutionary Bordeaux.* Oxford: Clarendon Press.

Forrest, Alan 1981: *The French Revolution and the poor.* Oxford: Basil Blackwell.

Forrest, Alan 1989: *Conscripts and deserters: the army and French society during the Revolution and Empire.* New York: Oxford University Press.

Forrest, Alan 1990: *Soldiers of the French Revolution.* Durham, NC: Duke University Press.

Forrest, Alan and Jones, Peter (eds) 1991: *Reshaping France: town, country and region during the French Revolution.* Manchester: Manchester University Press.

Forster, Robert 1960: *The nobility of Toulouse in the eighteenth century.* Baltimore: Johns Hopkins University Press.

Furet, François 1981: *Interpreting the French Revolution.* Cambridge: Cambridge University Press.

Furet, François 1992: *Revolutionary France, 1770–1880.* Oxford: Basil Blackwell.

Furet, François and Ozouf, Mona (eds) 1990: *A Critical Dictionary of the French Revolution.* Cambridge, Mass.: Harvard University Press.

Garrioch, David 1986: *Neighbourhood and community in Paris, 1740–1790.* Cambridge: Cambridge University Press.

Gendron, François 1979: *La jeunesse dorée: episodes de la Révolution française.* Québec: Presses de l'Université du Québec.

Gobry, Ivan 1991: *Joseph Le Bon: La Terreur dans le nord de la France.* Paris: Mercure de France.

Godechot, Jacques 1970: *The taking of the Bastille.* London: Faber & Faber.

Godechot, Jacques 1971: *The counter-revolution, doctrine and action* (tr. Salvator Artanasio). Princeton: Princeton University Press.

Goodwin, Albert 1953: *The French Revolution*. London: Hutchinson.

Gough, Hugh 1988: *The newspaper press in the French Revolution*. London: Routledge.

Greer, Donald 1935: *The incidence of the Terror during the French Revolution*. Cambridge, Mass.: Harvard University Press.

Griffiths, Robert 1988: *Le centre perdu: Malouet et les 'monarchiens' dans la Révolution française*. Grenoble: Presses Universitaires de Grenoble.

Guilhaumou, Jacques 1989: 'Discourse and revolution: the foundation of political language, 1789–92'. In G. Levitine (ed.) *Culture and revolution: cultural ramifications of the French Revolution*. College Park: University of Maryland at College Park, 118–33.

Hampson, Norman 1974: *The life and times of Maximilien Robespierre*. Oxford: Basil Blackwell.

Hampson, Norman 1978: *Danton*. Oxford: Basil Blackwell.

Hampson, Norman 1981: *The Terror in the French Revolution*. London: Historical Association.

Hampson, Norman 1991: *Saint-Just*. Oxford: Basil Blackwell.

Hanson, Paul 1989: *Provincial politics in the French Revolution: Caen and Limoges, 1789–1794*. Baton Rouge: Louisiana State University Press.

Hardman, John 1973: *French Revolution Documents*, vol. 2 (1792–5). Oxford: Basil Blackwell.

Hesse, Carla 1991: *Publishing and cultural politics in revolutionary Paris, 1789–1810*. Berkeley: University of California Press.

Higonnet, Patrice 1981: *Class, ideology and the rights of nobles during the French Revolution*. Oxford: Clarendon Press.

Hirsch, Jean-Pierre 1990: 'L'imbroglio révolutionnaire: conflits et consensus'. In J. Juillard (ed.), *Histoire de France: l'État et ses conflits*. Paris: Seuil, 207–63.

Hufton, Olwen 1974: *The poor of eighteenth-century France*. Oxford: Clarendon Press.

Hufton, Olwen 1992: *Women and the limits of citizenship in the French Revolution*. Toronto: University of Toronto Press.

Hunt, Lynn 1984: *Politics, culture and class in the French Revolution*. Berkeley: University of California Press.

Hutt, Maurice 1983: *Chouannerie and counter-revolution: Puisaye, the princes and the British government in the 1790s*. 2 vols. Cambridge: Cambridge University Press.

Jones, Peter 1988: *The peasantry in the French Revolution*. Cambridge: Cambridge University Press.

Kaplan, Steven 1982: *The famine plot persuasion in eighteenth-century France*. Philadelphia: American Philosophical Society.

Kaplan, Steven 1993: *Adieu 89*. Paris: Fayard.

Kates, Gary 1985: *The Cercle Social, the Girondins, and the French Revolution*. Princeton: Princeton University Press.

Kennedy, Michael 1982–88: *The Jacobin clubs in the French Revolution*. 2 vols. Princeton: Princeton University Press.

Laffon, J.-B. and Soulet, J.-F. 1982: *Histoire de Tarbes*. Roanne: Horvath.

Lefebvre, Georges 1932: *La Grande Peur de 1789*. Paris: Armand Colin.

Lefebvre, Georges 1939: *The coming of the French Revolution* (tr. Robert Palmer). Princeton: Princeton University Press.

Lefebvre, Georges 1962–4: *The French Revolution* (tr. Elizabeth Moss Evanson). 2 vols. London: Routledge & Kegan Paul.

Le Goff, T. J. A. 1981: *Vannes and its region. a study of town and country in eighteenth-century France. Oxford: Clarendon Press*.

Leith, James 1989: 'On the religiosity of the French Revolution'. In G. Levitine (ed.) *Culture and Revolution: Cultural Ramifications of the French Revolution*. College Park: University of Maryland at College Park, 171–85.

Levy, Darline Gay, Applewhite, Harriet Branson, and Johnson, Mary Durham 1979: *Women in revolutionary Paris, 1789–95*. Urbana: University of Illinois Press.

Lewis, Gwynne 1978: *The second vendée: the continuity of counter-revolution in the Department of the Gard, 1789–1815*. Oxford: Clarendon Press.

Lewis, Gwynne 1993: *The French Revolution: rethinking the debate*. London: Routledge.

Lewis, Gwynne and Lucas, Colin (eds) 1983: *Beyond the Terror: essays in French regional and social history, 1794–1815*. Cambridge: Cambridge University Press.

Lucas, Colin 1973: *The structure of the Terror: the example of Javogues and the Loire*. Oxford: Clarendon Press.

Lucas, Colin (ed.) 1988: *The political culture of the French Revolution* Oxford: Pergamon Press.

Lucas, Colin (ed.) 1991: *Rewriting the French Revolution*. Oxford: Clarendon Press.

McManners, John 1969: *The French Revolution and the Church*. London: SPCK.

Markov, Walter and Soboul, Albert 1957: *Die Sansculotten von Paris: Dokumente zur Geschichte der Volksbewegung, 1793–94*. East Berlin: Akademie Verlag.

Melzer, Sara E. and Rabine, Leslie W. 1992: *Rebel daughters: women and the French Revolution*. New York: Oxford University Press.

Montpellier 1988: *Les pratiques politiques en province à l'époque de la Révolution française*. Montpellier: Université Paul-Valéry, Centre d'histoire contemporaine du Languedoc méditerranéan et du Roussillon.

Nicolas, Jean (ed.) 1985: *Mouvements populaires et conscience sociale, XVIe–XIXe siècles*. Paris: Maloine.

Nieto, Philippe 1988: *Le centenaire de la Révolution dauphinoise*. Grenoble: Presses Universitaires de Grenoble.

Ozouf, Mona 1988: *Festivals and the French Revolution* (tr. Alan Sheridan). Cambridge, Mass.: Harvard University Press.

Ozouf-Marignier, Marie-Vic 1989: *La formation des départements*. Paris: Editions de l'Ecole des Hautes Etudes en Sciences Sociales.

Patrick, Alison 1972: *The men of the First French Republic*. Baltimore: Johns Hopkins University Press.

Phillips, Roderick 1981: *Family breakdown in late eighteenth-century France*. Oxford: Clarendon Press.

Roberts, Warren 1989: *Jacques-Louis David, revolutionary artist*. Chapel Hill: University of North Carolina Press.

Rose, R. B. 1978: *Gracchus Babeuf: The First Revolutionary Communist*. Stanford: Stanford University Press.

Schama, Simon 1989: *Citizens: a chronicle of the French Revolution*. New York: Viking.

Scott, Samuel 1978: *The response of the royal army to the French Revolution*. Oxford: Clarendon Press.

Scott, William 1973: *Terror and repression in revolutionary Marseilles*. London: Macmillan.

Secher, Reynald 1986: *Le génocide franco-français: la Vendée-vengé*. Paris: Presses Universitaires de France.

Soboul, Albert 1959: *Les soldats de l'an II*. Paris: Livre Club Diderot.

Soboul, Albert 1974: *The French Revolution, 1787–99* (tr. Alan Forrest and Colin Jones). London: New Left Books.

Sonenscher, Michael 1989: *Work and wages: natural law, politics and the eighteenth-century French trades*. Cambridge: Cambridge University Press.

Stephens, H. Morse 1892: *Orators of the French Revolution*. 2 vols. Oxford: Clarendon Press.

Stewart, John Hall (ed.) 1951: *A documentary history of the French Revolution.* New York: Macmillan.

Sutherland, D. M. G. 1982: *The Chouans: the social origins of popular counter-revolution in upper Brittany, 1770–1796.* Oxford: Clarendon Press.

Sutherland, D. M. G. 1985: *France, 1789–1815: Revolution and counter-revolution.* London: Collins.

Tackett, Timothy 1986: *Religion, revolution and regional culture in eighteenth-century France: the Ecclesiastical Oath of 1791.* Princeton: Princeton University Press.

Thompson, J. M. 1935: *Robespierre.* Oxford: Basil Blackwell.

Tulard, Jean 1985: *Napoleon: the myth of the saviour* (tr. Teresa Waugh). London: Methuen.

Vovelle, Michel (ed.) 1989: *L'image de la Révolution Française.* 4 vols. Oxford: Pergamon Press.

Vovelle, Michel 1991: *The Revolution against the Church: from reason to the supreme being.* Cambridge: Polity Press.

Vovelle, Michel 1993: *Combats pour la Révolution Française.* Paris: La Découverte.

Woloch, Isser 1970: *Jacobin legacy: the democratic movement under the Directory.* Princeton: Princeton University Press.

Glossary

Abbé – Abbot; also an honorary title given to clergymen.

Agences de commerce – Commercial agencies created by the revolutionary government in order to exercise greater control over trade and commerce.

Agent national – Post created by law of 14 *frimaire* II to extend government control over the district and municipal councils; the *agent national* replaced the old municipal prosecutor and was directly answerable to Paris.

Ancien Régime – Old regime; a term invented by the Revolutionaries to distinguish the new order from what had existed before 1789.

Anobli – A commoner who had bought nobility or who had been ennobled for his service to the state.

Armées révolutionnaires – The so-called 'people's armies' of radical militants, established in 1793 in Paris and in some parts of the provinces to enforce revolutionary laws and take terror into the countryside; in Paris they were dominated by the radical sections and were responsible for dechristianizing the surrounding countryside and for enforcing requisitions.

Assignat – The paper currency introduced in 1790 to replace specie for commercial transactions; its value was theoretically secured against the sale of national lands, but in fact it suffered catastrophic depreciation until by 1795 it had become virtually worthless.

Avocats au parlement – Barristers to the Parlement of Paris; they formed a powerful corporation at the end of the *ancien régime*.

Bailliage – Area of jurisdiction of certain of the royal courts at the end of the *ancien régime*.

Bienfaisance – Philanthropy, poor relief; in revolutionary eyes this had a humanitarian rather than a religious or charitable connotation.

Biens nationaux – National lands; the property of the Church, the Crown and of *émigrés* which was confiscated by the state at various times between 1789 and 1792 and was subsequently sold off to finance the war effort.

Bonnet rouge – The red Phrygian cap which became a symbol of the Parisian sans-culottes and subsequently of the Republic itself.

Brumaire – The *coup d'état* of 1799 (18 *brumaire* VII) which overthrew the Directory and brought Napoleon to power.

Cadastre – Cadastral survey or plan, showing the exact extent and relationship of buildings and property; a strict mathematical measure for the division of the territory.

Cahiers de doléances – Lists of grievances which were drawn up at every level from parish to province in preparation for the meeting of the Estates-General.

Chef-lieu – The administrative centre at every level of administration (canton, district, department).

Chouan – Peasant insurgent in Brittany and parts of the west; so called because of the owl-like cries through which they communicated from hamlet to hamlet in the dispersed habitat of rural Brittany.

Chouannerie – Term used to describe the counter-revolutionary movement in Brittany and the guerrilla tactics they used against the French state.

Citoyens actifs – 'Active citizens'; those who were recognized by the 1791 constitution as having the necessary qualifications to vote; those who lacked the necessary income (measured by the amount paid in taxes) were known as 'passive citizens' (or *citoyens passifs*).

Colonnes infernales – The so-called 'infernal columns'; under Turreau and other generals, used in the Vendée to spread fear and destruction in the population.

Colonnes mobiles – Units sent in to rural areas to root out deserters and counter-revolutionaries.

Commissaires – Envoys, commissioners, entrusted by Paris with a particular responsibility; there were, for example, *commissaires* sent to the armies in 1793 to oversee the war effort, and others sent to the departments to ensure that policing measures were being stringently enforced.

Compagnonnages – Journeymen's organizations, which looked after the interests of workers and craftsmen and organized apprenticeships in many eighteenth-century trades.

Conseil des Anciens – Council of Elders under the Directory; the *anciens* had to be aged at least forty, and the council could change laws passed to it by the lower house if it found them inappropriate.

Conseil des Cinq-Cents – Council of Five Hundred, the lower house under the Directory; its members had to be aged at least thirty, and they had the job of voting 'resolutions' which formed the basis for legislation.

Corporations – Gilds; these were the craft organisations, dominated by master craftsmen, which controlled the trades within each city in *ancien régime* France.

Curé – Parish priest, a clergyman holding cure of souls *(curé)*.

Découpage – The division of the territory into its new revolutionary units of administration (departments, districts, communes); this was effected, after much squabbling, in 1790.

Débaptisation – Renaming, or 'debaptizing', of villages, streets and people which accompanied the dechristianizing campaign of 1793–4.

Département – Department, the principal administrative division of France after 1790 when the old provinces were abolished; the land area of France was divided into eighty-three departments, though the number would increase with the annexation of the Comtat Venaissin in 1790 and the subdivision of the Rhône-et-Loire in 1793.

Diocèse – Diocese, unit of ecclesiastical administration; their rationalization and reorganization in the Civil Constitution of the Clergy was an important element in causing the conflict between the Revolution and the Catholic Church.

Émigrés – Those who emigrated from France to escape from the Revolution; many, though not all, were nobles and clerics, and the law prescribed increasingly harsh penalties for those who returned.

Faubourgs – Suburbs, areas lying outwith the city walls; the Paris *faubourgs* – most notably the Faubourg Saint-Antoine and the Faubourg Saint-Marcel – were to be among the most radical areas of popular politics during the 1790s.

Fédération – Celebration of patriotism and unity; the first *fédérations* were held in provincial centres in late 1789 and early 1790, and the movement culminated in the great festival in Paris on 14 July 1789 which brought together national guardsmen from all over France (the *Fête de la Fédération*).

Fédérés – Those who came to Paris from the provinces to represent their cities and departments at the national *Fête de la Fédération* on 14 July; in 1792 many of them would stay on in the capital after the festival, and their presence was crucial on 10 August when the Tuileries was stormed and Louis XVI overthrown.

Fructidor – The *coup d'état* of 1797 (18 *fructidor* V) by which the Directory and the Councils were purged of royalist sympathizers.

Généralité – Unit of government under the *ancien régime*, used principally for tax collection and fiscal administration.

Gens sans aveu – People to be treated with suspicion since no respectable member of the community could be found to vouch for them; a perennial category of suspect in eighteenth-century policing.

Germinal – Failed popular rising in Paris in the spring of 1795, one of the last *journées* staged by the radical sections (13 *Germinal* III).

Gouvernement – Military unit of administration under the *ancien régime*.

Grande Peur – Great Fear, the panic which swept some regions of France in response to peasant violence and *châteaux* burning in the summer of 1789.

Insoumission – Draft dodgers, conscripts who evaded military service.

Jacquerie – Outburst of peasant violence, a traditional form of rural protest.

Jeunesse dorée – The 'Gilded Youth'; right-wing youth movement which formed after Thermidor in Paris and the larger provincial cities, which adopted the lifestyle of ostentatious dandies and took pleasure in beating up known Jacobins and those who had assisted them during the Terror.

Journée – A 'day' of popular revolutionary action in Paris; the term is reserved for the great days of radical violence, like 14 July 1789 or 10 August 1792 which helped to change the direction of the Revolution.

Laboureur – A rich peasant; someone of substance in rural society in that he would own a plough and might hire the labour of others.

Légion d'honneur – Legion of Honour, created by Napoleon to reward personal service or service to the state.

Lettre de cachet – Letter signed by the King ordering the arrest and immediate imprisonment of a subject; the practice was regarded as one of the principal abuses of royal power and its abolition was widely demanded in the *cahiers de doléances* in 1789.

Levée des 300,000 – Law of 24 February 1793 ordering the raising of 300,000 additional soldiers for the armies; quotas were allocated to each district, but the method of recruitment was left to local choice.

Levée en masse – Law of 23 August 1793 mobilizing the entire French nation for war until such time as peace was signed.

Lit de justice – Formal session of the Parlement called so that the King could override the objections of the *parlementaires* and impose a law by royal edict.

Livres rouges – Printed lists of the names, addresses and crimes of local terrorists distributed after Thermidor as a measure of White Terror, especially in the departments of the Midi.

Mandat territorial – New form of paper currency introduced in 1796 after the calamitous depreciation of the *assignat*; this, too, rapidly lost value and was abandoned in the spring of 1797.

Maréchaussée – The police force of the *ancien régime*, organized and paid for nationally under the authority of the Marshals of

France; in 1790 it would be abolished and replaced by the *gendarmerie*.

Maximum – Laws which sought to impose fixed prices, first for grain, then (in the General Maximum of 29 September 1793) on all goods deemed to be of prime necessity.

Menu peuple – The poor, the common people, the crowd in the towns.

Monarchiens – Deputies to the Constituent Assembly who formed themselves into a pro-monarchist faction in 1789 and 1790, advocating a constitutional monarchy rather on the English model.

Municipalité – Mayor and municipal officers who were charged with the administration of each commune.

Muscadins – Fops, dandies, those who ostentatiously adhered to the *jeunesse dorée* in the months after Thermidor.

Nonante-cinq – 1795, the current Parisian form of what would now be 'Quatre-vingt-quinze'; so severe was the weather and so great the suffering in the winter of 1795 that 'Nonante-cinq' came to symbolize popular misery.

Notables – Men of substance and standing in the local community to whom local power increasingly passed.

Octrois – Tolls imposed on all goods entering a town or city, abolished by the Revolution in 1791; the tolls were blamed for high food prices and the *octroi* gates had become a target for popular anger, especially in Paris.

Pacte de famine – Conspiracy between aristocrats, wholesalers, merchants, and even millers to hold back corn supplies from the market in order to force up prices and starve the poor into submission; allegations of a *pacte de famine*, involving even the royal family, were a common theme of popular demonology.

Parlement – One of the thirteen sovereign courts of *ancien régime* France. They were the supreme court of appeal within the area of their jurisdiction; they also claimed political rights, like the right of remonstrance, and had to register royal edicts before they became law.

Parlementaire – Member of a Parlement; in Paris and major provincial cities a powerful legal elite had emerged by the end of the *ancien régime*, ennobled by virtue of their office; especially in Paris the *parlementaires* were a major focus of opposition to the Crown.

Partage – Division of the common lands among individual peasants; in 1792–3 there was considerable popular agitation in certain parts of France for the introduction of *partage*, but elsewhere the viability of the countryside depended on the maintenance of the commons.

Patrie en danger – The clarion call to defend the Revolution against its enemies; the declaration of the 'Patrie en danger' heralded the introduction of emergency measures and the denial of individual liberties.

Patriotes – Patriots, the name given to those who in 1788 and 1789 attacked the Parlements and identified themselves with new and advanced ideas.

Pays d'élection – Administrative description under the *ancien régime* of those provinces which did not have their own estates and where tax administration was organized directly by the Intendant.

Pays de petite culture – Areas where there was little large-scale farming and where agriculture was largely organized on a subsistence basis.

Philosophes – Writers of the Enlightenment whose humanism was admired by many of the Revolutionaries and whose persistent questioning was deemed to have undermined many of the institutions of the *ancien régime*.

Prairial – Popular *journée* of May 1795 in Paris, which was rapidly crushed by the authorities.

Prévôt des marchands – Principal municipal administrator in Paris during the *ancien régime*.

Roturier – Commoner.

Sans-culottes – Popular militants of the Paris sections; by 1793 the term was used more widely to describe those who had egalitarian and republican ideas.

Séance royale – Session of the Parlement of Paris, and subsequently of the Estates-General, where the members assembled in the presence of the King to hear an important royal statement of policy.

Sectionnaires – Those who attended sectional meetings; popular militants.

Sections – Administrative divisions of Paris and the larger provincial cities established with the municipal reforms of 1790 (there were, for instance, 48 in Paris and 32 in Lyon); sections increasingly claimed political rights, including the right to sit in permanent session, and became a forum for popular politics.

Seigneur – Lord of the manor, noble to whom various forms of feudal obligation were due.

Taxation populaire – A 'fair' price, often fixed quite arbitrarily by the crowd, at which merchants and stall owners would be forced to sell their wares.

Thermidor – The *journée* of 9 *thermidor* II (27 July 1794) which led to the fall of Robespierre and ended the Jacobin Republic; Robespierre and his closest associates were summarily condemned and executed on the following day.

Tour de France – Traditional part of the eighteenth-century apprenticeship in many trades, whereby the young worker would move from employer to employer and from town to town learning different aspects of his craft.

Vendée militaire – The area of western France affected by counter-revolution in the spring of 1793. In all, six departments rose in rebellion against the Republic, including the Vendée itself; the term 'Vendée militaire' is used to identify this larger region of insurrection.

Vendémiaire – Right-wing insurrection in Paris in 1795, which enjoyed a considerable degree of popular support.

Ventôse Decrees – A series of laws which sought to redistribute the property of enemies of the Revolution; they were strongly egalitarian in tone and to many smacked of vengeance and class war.

Index

Note: Page numbers in italics refer to figures.

183